Abandoned!

...A Jewish Wife's True Story

ANONYMOUS

MIRKOV PUBLICATIONS, INC.
Pittsburgh, Pennsylvania

MIRKOV PUBLICATIONS,INC.
P.O. Box 81971
Pittsburgh, Pennsylvania 15217
1-(800)-851-8303

Copyright © 1998 by Anonymous

Library of Congress Catalog Card Number 98-068408

10 9 8 7 6 5 4 3 2 1

ISBN 0-9648508-3-4

Manufactured in the United States of America

Table of Contents

Dedication

With all my heart and love, this book is dedicated to my two beautiful children. First, my beautiful, righteous, *Torah*-loving daughter whom I can't thank enough. I made her suffer more than her share of heartache during my traumatic illness and I truly believe that her constant prayers to G-d brought me a quick recovery. My experience will definitely allow me to fulfill my goal of building my own "Orthodox Abuse Center," a place for Orthodox women who find themselves trapped in a marriage with a mentally ill spouse as well as other problems. My prayers to G-d to send my daughter a wonderful, loving, and *Torah*-loving husband of excellent character were answered. I am now enjoying the fruits of that marriage and a daughter who is an *ezer* to her husband who deserves her, and their healthy, fantastic, magnificent little blessings, my grandchildren. Thank G-d!

I want you to know that I am very proud of you and I love you very much. I pray that you and your wonderful family will have one hundred and twenty years together with me and your brother and his family, with G-d's help in health, happiness, and *parnassa*.

I also dedicate this book to my beloved, wonderful, *talmid chochem* son whose fervent prayers also helped me through my nightmarish illness, for which I thank you. I pray to G-d that you and your beautiful family will have one hundred and twenty years together with me and your sister and her family with G-d's help in health, happiness, and *parnassa*.

I am very proud of you and your beautiful wife and little blessings, my grandchildren, and I thank G-d that I have beautiful,

Torah-loving grandchildren from both of my fantastic, magnificent children. I wish you all with G-d's help continued good health and *parnassa*.

A very special "*yasher koach*" also to my very devoted friend, C.S. who was always there when I needed her.

My thanks to those who helped make this book a reality: M.L.S., S.W., M.K.,R.F., Rabbi and Mrs. B.H., Rabbi and Mrs. M.H., Ailene S., who from the bottom of her heart helped me write this book and gave me such helpful advice; Lea S., who designed the original front cover; Bernie M., who helped with the computer, and I am truly indebted to my priceless and patient first editor, Erica Meyer Rauzin, who worked very hard with love and spent endless hours preparing the original manuscript. I am grateful to Marcia Goldman of Mirkov Publications whose efforts and talents made this new edition possible.

A very special thanks to Dr. A. Norman Goldwasser of Horizon Psychological Services, for his most invaluable, sagacious advice and direction. *Yasher koach.*

Last, but not least, I wish to thank all my loyal and wonderful friends for caring and helping me through the most difficult crisis of my life. You all know who you are. To my wonderful doctors, I can only say, "Thanks a lot from the bottom of my heart."

Anonymous

Foreword

In her gripping personal account of marital discord and emotional abuse, Anonymous speaks from the heart in an effort to *mechazek* and encourage women who are in dysfunctional marriages. True, "Abandoned" is about pain, struggle, and disappointment; but it is also a story of strength, resilience, and courage. This is a story of a woman determined to not just survive, but to thrive in the face of domestic disaster. Through *bitachon* and perseverance, she was able to raise children who are whole in every respect, despite the overwhelming odds against her.

This is an important contribution to the understanding of pathological relationships, and of how, from a *Torah* perspective, one can overcome the difficulties inherent in a marriage that cannot work. Women can and do survive divorce, and have the ability to make new lives for themselves and their children. Although it is certainly traumatic for all concerned, there is a reason why the *Torah* provides for a *krisus*, a cutting off of the unsalvageable marriage. Women are entitled, *al pi halacha*, to have relationships with their husbands that are based on respect, emotional support, and love. Devoid of all these, a marriage is not a marriage, and should be terminated. "Abandoned" should be able to provide a woman in such a situation the strength to get the help she needs and to make the necessary changes in her life and the lives of her children, if there is no hope for a change in the marriage.

It is my fervent hope that through the efforts of individuals such as the author, women who are trapped can free themselves, and those who are embarking on a search for their *zivug* will look more carefully, so that future disasters can be prevented. Ultimately, let us all be *mispallel* that we can work together to promote *shalom bayis* for all of *Klal Yisrael*, for ourselves and for generations to come.

Dr. A. Norman Goldwasser
Miami Beach, Florida

Introduction

The saddest woman is a woman in an unhappy marriage.

My story is for Orthodox women who find themselves, through no fault of their own, trapped in unhealthy, abusive marriages. My advice, based on hard won experience, is meant to motivate them to assess their situation. To adapt the old saying, I hope to convey to them the ability to change their situation if it can be changed, the strength to accept it if it can be accepted, and the wisdom to know the difference.

In our holy *Ketubah,* the groom declares to the bride:

"Be thou my wife according to the law of Moses and Israel. I faithfully promise that I will be a true husband unto thee. I will honor and cherish thee. I will work for thee; I will protect and support thee; and will provide all that is necessary for thy sustenance even as it beseemeth a Jewish husband to do. I also take upon myself further obligations for thy maintenance as are prescribed by our religious statutes. The said bride has plighted her troth unto him in affection and in sincerity."

With the above promise by every Jewish groom, "WHY THE ABUSE?" What is the cause of this disease that has filtered through to the Orthodox community, which used to be a role model of family values to the world? With intense research by Orthodox therapists, psychologists, rabbis and psychiatrists, a solution to this problem will be found.

This book tries to answer that question. This book is the story of a beautiful young Orthodox woman who found herself caught up with a very emotionally and mentally ill man, who since the cradle was raised by an emotionally starved, ignorant, miserable, destructive, selfish woman whom he called "Mamale." This "Mamale" destroyed both of her sons' marriages and instilled in them an Oedipus Complex that was beyond therapy. The young wife literally grabbed her two children and ran from her unhealthy situation to a beautiful life of health, happiness and success. With the help of G-d, she had a deep sense of *bitachon* and *emunah*. She singlehandedly raised her two children to be successful, healthy, productive and happily married parents. Her son is a *talmid chochem* and her daughter is a *zadekes*. They are both continuing the Orthodox way of life and their children are the continuing link in the unbroken chain of Judaism.

The wife worked very hard to be able to give her children a beautiful home, dress them and herself beautifully, entertained, and enjoyed endless friendships. She traveled with her children. Until this day, their friends come into her house and talk about the wonderful memories of *Shabbosim* and *yom tovim* they shared together. Raising an Orthodox son is not an easy task without a male role model, but with G-d's help this mother survived all the odds and turned out a son who is a true *ben-Torah*. Her beautiful daughter was the most popular throughout her school years, and everywhere she goes, she is loved. Her son was the top man at his *yeshiva* and was also very popular among his friends and *Rabbonim*.

I AM THAT WIFE. My name is Anonymous, at least that

is my pen name. My real name is my last secret, withheld to protect the privacy of my children. The names I have used in this book are all fictitious but the characters and situations are authentic. This is the life I led.

If you want to get in touch with me please contact the publisher who will forward your letters to me. I hope my book will give you all the strength you need to go ahead with your own plans for the future.

A List of DO'S

You, the Orthodox woman trapped in a marriage with an ill husband, can also be successful. All you need is a deep sense of *bitochon* and *emunah* in G-d. **GET OUT** of your unhealthy situation. A beautiful world is out there waiting for you to constructively contribute to it.

The following is a list of DO's to help you cope with your stressful situation and also help you keep up your self-esteem and self-respect until the time comes when you will be ready and able to solve your problem.

1.   **First and foremost, take a good look at yourself in the mirror.** Remember with pride that you are, with G-d's help, the rock your children depend upon. You are their role model, their father and mother, their only source of adult love and stability. You **must,** and I mean **must,** maintain your dignity. The first step is to maintain your appearance. Your dress or robe should be spotless. Your shoes should be attractive. Your hair or *sheitel* must be nicely styled. Put on make-up; keep your manicure and pedicure in good condition, no chipped nails or nail polish. All of this will help you

cope, and will give you a sense of pride and a feeling of self esteem.

2.   Your home is an extension of yourself, a spotless house is the order of the day, and a comfortable and loving environment for your children. Toys on the floor are a blessing. Also, keep your children neat and clean. Their clothes should fit. They should be taught respect for the furniture and their possessions. Again, nothing has to be expensive, just clean and in good taste, so that the children can be proud when they have their friends over.

3.   Associate only with happy people and invite plenty of friends to your home. You should not spend too much time alone. Maintain a sense of humor, keep laughing and smiling. Remember that everything in life is *bashert*.

4.   Never discuss your problems with your friends, for two reasons. First, it can backfire and your children will be embarrassed when their friends tell them what they overheard their parents saying about your problems. Second, they are not professional counselors and might turn out to be *yentas* who can't even solve their own problems. Seek an understanding *Rabbi* or a constructive therapist, or even a teacher from one of your children's *yeshivos.* They are better equipped to help you from an objective standpoint.

5.   Remember, if a mother is happy, her children are happy, no matter where you live. If you are miserable in a mansion, the whole environment suffers. If you are happy in a small apartment, it's contagious.

6.   Kiss and hug your children constantly and tell them you love them.

7.   Do happy and fun things with them.

8.   Always tell your children that they are your blessings and that they are not responsible for what is happening.

9.   Tell your children constantly how lucky you are to be their mother and how you love and adore them. They need to hear it. Let them speak openly about their father without any negative comments from you.

10.   Encourage them to cry when they need to, but only in front of you.

11.   If you feel your children need a male role model, try to chose a fine childless *frum* couple whom you can adopt as foster grandparents.

12.   Prepare your sons and daughters to make a living and be independent and self-supporting. Don't push your daughter to marry because her friends are, or because it is the thing to do. Let your children enjoy their teen years, learning, relaxing with friends, going to school, getting a job, traveling and participating in experiences that build maturity and enable them to learn to make their own decisions. Teach them to handle their own finances; get them ready for marriage and parenthood. If they ever need to become the sole supporter of their family, they should be able and prepared, capable of earning a living and of shouldering the responsibilities of raising children.

Now for the Don'ts:

1.   Don't burden your children with your problems. They're not mature enough to understand your plight and they certainly will be having their own problems. Remember the man you despise is their father and he is a part of them. If they hear you talk against him they will think you don't like them, and you don't want depressed children. If they ask why he is not living with them, tell them something that will suffice for the moment. When they are older, they will make their own decisions.

2.   Don't cry in front of your children. It is a sign of weakness and it will affect their emotional security. Your children should always see you happy. Cry alone when they are not around. You are their Rock of Gibraltar. They draw strength from you; you are their father and mother.

3.   Don't take your anger at your ex-husband's actions out on your children.

4.   Don't dwell on negative past memories. It's self-destructive. Discuss everything with your professional problem-solver, if you need one.

5.   Don't channel your energies in negative ways. Do not harp on the fact that what is happening to you is not what you deserve. Accept the fact that this is pre-destined and you have to resolve this crisis. Everyone has a portion in life. Channel your feelings in a positive way.

      6.   **If your ex-husband wants to pick a fight, do not lower yourself to his level.** The less contact you have with him, the healthier for you and your children. You know fighting doesn't solve anything and is part of his abusive behavior. He takes pleasure in seeing you get upset. Do not channel your energy destructively.

7.   **Don't ask yourself "Why did this happen to me?"** It's bashert that you were to bring your children into this world to continue the chain of Judaism; they were meant to be born. Perhaps you were fulfilling some other mission. Stay strong. Keep your head up. Like Jewish women throughtout our history, you are the source of family strength.

      Have *bitochon* and *emunah* in G-d and believe you're going to survive and be successful. And many years later, as you look back, you will see that everything was for the best. We all have a portion to fulfill in life and thank G-d, He doesn't give us anything we cannot handle. If G-d selects us to be involved with abuse and single parenthood, He will also give us the strength to survive. Perhaps in my case, if I had had a normal marriage, I would not be aware that there is a need for an Orthodox Abuse Center to help other women.

      King Solomon put it brilliantly: **The happiest person is one who is happy with his or her own lot.** Trouble makes one stronger. All through the *Torah*, our leaders have been tested by G-d, and have overcome, and have instilled their strength in *K'lal Yisrael*. Remember that the women throughout our history have been the strength of *K'lal Yisrael*.

Fundamental *Torah* Ideology

Our holy *Torah* not only condones divorce but actually advocates divorce in circumstances where there is no domestic harmony, stemming either from mental, physical, sexual or emotional abuse against a wife.

The *Torah* is very concerned with domestic harmony (*shalom bayis*), an ideal which is not easy to achieve. After the courtship and the wedding ceremony, once a couple is united and begins to live together, they begin to understand the differences between them in sexuality, upbringing, personality, character traits, value systems, priorities and needs. The woman begins to see her spouse's virtues and, unfortunately, his short-comings, and vice-versa. Our *Torah* is the blueprint for the sacredness of our marriages. The *Torah* asks a man to honor his wife, love and cherish her, cling to her, respect her and place her first before all his other relatives and commitments.

Our *Torah* does not look down upon a woman as a "lesser" being in comparison to her husband. Wife and husband are equal, although they have different missions to fulfill. G-d told Adam that woman was created so he would not be alone, so he would have a help-mate. She will be his *ezer-knegdo,* which means if he is deserving of her, she will bend over backwards to please him and make him happy, and fulfill his every wish. However, if he is not deserving of her, she will go out of her way to be his *knegdo*, and make his life miserable.

Women were created to bring strength, power, and a sixth sense about emotion and intuition to a marriage, not to serve as outlets for their husband's emotional anger, sexual passion or physical fury. Sexual union was created as an act of love and procreation, imbued with purity and holiness, not as an act of violence. Marriage was created as a haven away from the world, not an outlet for pent-up rage and emotional turmoil.

G-d entrusted women with some difficult commandments and responsibilities: keeping a kosher home, bringing up children in a *Torah* true way, making the home a spiritual, loving environment and, above all, being a role model to instill constructive spirituality in children as a blueprint for their adult lives. He also endowed women with sacred laws concerning family purity (*taharat-hamishpacha*), a code which leads to domestic harmony, a happy Jewish marriage and a home filled with contentment.

How wise our holy *Torah* and scholarly Rabbis were. The *Torah* is very concerned with a mutually gratifying sexual relationship as a very important part of domestic harmony. The laws of family purity deal with monthly physical and sexual abstinence for a minimum of twelve days from the onset of menstruation, (until the woman, after being without any menstrual flow for seven days), submerges herself in the spiritually purifying ritual bath (*mikvah*). During the time of separation, the woman and her husband are to abstain from all physical and sexual contact. In the right circumstances, this is a time of great closeness, as couples endeavor to verbalize their deepest feelings and share their lives without touching.

In a loving, devoted marriage, the first union after abstention is beautiful, a recreation of the first night a bride and groom spent together. The passionate desire and excitement that accompany the end of separation combines with the husband's joyous fulfillment of his duty to satisfy his wife's needs, even above his own. This is a stated commandment, a *mitzvah*, and the reward for keeping it is marital happiness and mutual devotion. This is the way a Jewish man and woman are supposed to lead their lives together, according to the *Torah*.

However, if a marriage is not lived in accordance with

Torah, but is instead destroyed with abuse, neglect, insults and violence, unfortunately an entirely different set of Biblical laws must be followed.

In Genesis, Chapter 2, lines 17 and 18, we read,

"G-d said man's being alone is not good. I will make him a help-mate. The man said, "This now is bone from my bones and flesh from my flesh. This will be called 'isha' for this was taken from 'ish'.

That is why G-d commands man to leave his father and his mother and cling to his wife and they become one flesh.

Marriage is a divine institution. Its sacred character dates back to the beginning of human society. Monogamy is the prototype of marriage instituted by G-d. It is written, *"He shall cling to his wife."* The word "cling" implies a permanent union permeated with fidelity. Although physically the stronger, it is the man who must "cling" to his wife, respecting her as his greatest treasure. In this way, the bonds of love which unite the couple will remain indestructible. A man's leaving his parents and clinging to his wife is the sacred Bible's recipe for the ultimate goal in marriage.

This commandment in no way obliterates the positive commandment, *"to honor one's father and mother"*. The *Torah* is telling us that a husband must make his loyalty and love for his WIFE first and foremost. This is possible to do simultaneously, while honoring parents, but it does not give the parents the right to control the lives of their children.

Usually in a "normal" marriage situation, the kinder you are to each other's parents, the greater the atmosphere of peace and togetherness and the less stress is found in the marriage. This glues the marriage together even more tightly. If the marriage is not a healthy marriage, destruction sets in instead of constructiveness.

This is a self-help manual. Every marital situation and the individuals involved vary. I wish there was a simple "rule of thumb" answer.

Unfortunately, no one can tell you what is the right thing to do in your situation. Only your individual feelings and depth of unhappiness, discomfort and distress can determine what you should do. Only you, alone, can come to the true realization of whether your marriage is over, or can be saved.

This book was not written to advocate divorce as the sole answer to an unhappy marriage. Rather, this book was written to let other Orthodox women know if they chose divorce, it is possible to be very successful as a single mother role model. Yes, a woman can find self-fulfillment without a male counterpart after divorce.

My overwhelming faith in G-d gave me continued strength to instill this deep faith into my children. My deep Judaic values played a very important part in my independent nature and gave me the strength to begin a new life with my children and to make a beautiful home for them.

✡✡✡

If you are the victim of spousal abuse, emotionally or physically, you can change your life. You can choose to be a content, divorced, single mother and role model. You can succeed alone. You can again achieve self-fulfillment and self-respect. And you can do it all as a *Torah*-true Jew. I did, and this book is my story.

I must begin with a word or two about my first goal: raising my children. After years of living with my husband Gershon, and his mother, Hodel, a destructive, mentally ill woman, I literally grabbed my son, Dovid, and my daughter, Avigail, and fled. With my deep sense of *bitochon* and *emunah* in G-d, we created a beautiful life of health, happiness and success. My children are now successful, happily married parents and I am now an independent, content grandmother living in the warmth of Florida.

Raising children without a father-male role model is not an easy task. Financially, I was below the poverty level, but I never, never felt poor due to my religious value system.

Today, my children and their children are continuing the unbroken link in the chain of Judaism. With G-d's help, Dovid is a true *ben-Torah*. He was a leader on his Yeshiva campus, well regarded by his friends and the *Rabbonim*. For his career, he chose *chinuch*, the rabbinate and *kiruv*.

My beautiful Avigail was popular and happy in school and is loved everywhere she goes. She excelled in special education. She worked for her husband for four years while he was in *kollel*, not easy with two little children. She is a gracious, loving *zadekes* (of course, this is her mother talking; I don't even pretend to be objective!).

Nonetheless, I worked hard to give my children a beautiful home. I dressed us well, we traveled together, we entertained and we enjoyed friendships with other people.

Since the day I left my ex-husband, I have had three driving goals: raise my two children, write this book, and open a much needed shelter for abused Orthodox women. I hope, with G-d's help, to build a place for Orthodox women and their children to flee to from unhealthy, abusive marriages.

My children are raised. My book is in your hands. My vision remains: a shelter where Orthodox women and their children can come for care and sustenance, a shelter for those who, today, are forced to remain in abusive, sick environments because they have nowhere else to go.

I am now working toward this vision, which is discussed in more detail in chapter eighteen. For now, let me tell you just a little about this dream, because I expect to make it a reality soon, with *Hashem's* help.

One day, with the help of G-d, an abused Orthodox woman will be able to call our shelter's eight hundred number for help, for clearance to board an airplane **gratis** and come to us in Florida to take shelter in a charming, comfortable, loving environment. I envision an institution that can provide food, clothing, and a clean room so victims can rest and regroup and begin therapy. I dream of a place where women can rebuild their self-esteem and that of their families, gaining self-respect by working as teachers in our *yeshiva*, as housekeepers, as cooks, as counselors, wherever their skills and training direct them. I hope to have a *yeshiva* for the children, a synagogue for daily prayers, a dining room, library, playroom, a safe haven where these women will feel at home. To escape abuse, they must first have somewhere to go.

When the Orthodox Abuse Center is ready, it will be advertised and I will notify everyone who has written to me. The ultimate goal of the center is to reunite families. There will be a staff of Orthodox professionals -- psychologists, therapists, psychiatrists, lawyers and Rabbis -- with two purposes: *to assist victims,* and *to study the roots of abuse* and the possible solutions to this erosion in the Orthodox family. Intense therapy may re-unite the families, which is also the goal of the center.

This is my dream. I wish you every fulfillment of your dreams, as well. Meanwhile, know that you can seize control of your own life. Be brave and believe in *Hashem*.

And now, for my story:

I will never forget watching my son as he was walking so proudly to *badek* his beautiful *kallah*. With my whole being, I prayed for the happiness and peace that fills his home today. But as he walked forward with his biological father and his future father-in-law, another refrain crept into the back of my mind, repeating, "I survived, I survived."

The beautiful, stimulating singing and music that accompanied him as he was to "*badek*" his beautiful *kallah* gave me a moment to steal a quick look at my beautiful daughter standing and clapping with a happy smile on her lovely face, wearing the magnificent lace dress she had designed. I couldn't prevent the quick memory, when only three short weeks earlier she had stood beside my hospital bed, her face tear-stained, praying for my quick recovery. I sent a silent prayer asking G-d to send her the best husband, happy, healthy children, and a happy family life for one hundred and twenty years. As I turned to watch my son, I repeated my prayer for him, and asked *Hashem* if I might also have one hundred and twenty years to enjoy my children and grandchildren. I would need that long, at least, to repay my daughter for all the emotional support she gave me during my traumatic illness. As the music surrounded me and thoughts of the hospital faded away, memory took over and suddenly, my mind flashed back to the train that long ago took me and my two little angels from the pits of despair to a future filled with sun, laughter, friends, love, security, health, happiness and, now, the joyous music of a wedding. This is our journey, and our story.

Chapter One: The Fatal Meeting

As a young, pretty, popular, gregarious middle-class Orthodox girl, I had more than my share of dates. I was just eighteen when I spent a week during the summer at a very prestigious kosher hotel in the Catskill Mountains. There, I met a presentable young man named Gershon. I continued to see him often at other social functions back in New York City. He was always overly polite. At every event, Gershon offered my friends and me a ride home even if our destination was miles out of his way. Even though we took advantage of his kindness, we really didn't notice how unusually quiet and shy he was. We learned he was a non-practicing Rabbi with his own business. We observed that he was a loner and that most of his friends were elderly and seemed more like acquaintances.

I was totally surprised to receive a letter from Gershon one day, asking if he could take me out the next time I came into the City. I answered it mainly out of pity, because I was not drawn to him. I told him I was planning to be in town the following week and would go out with him. Our date was a disaster, a silent bomb. In four hours, it seemed as if he spoke for a total of five seconds. He was too quiet for me; I wasn't interested.

Time passed and, a few years later, I bumped into Gershon again. He had not changed. He was still overly kind, overly quiet; getting him to talk was, in a cliché come to life, like pulling teeth. But my reaction to him had changed. As a chatty, out-going young woman, I found his quietness a virtue. Mistake number one.

My first assumption was that he was quiet because he was a good listener and genuinely interested in what I had to say. My second assumption was that he liked my outgoing personality; that the adage "opposites attract" was at work for us. He continued to offer rides to all our friends any time he could, so my third assumption was that he chauffeured people out of thoughtfulness and kindness. This led me to believe he was of good character.

No one ever told me anything negative about him. I never heard anything. I was never informed. Ironically, I was known as a perceptive person, as an excellent judge of character, but my assumptions were all wrong.

I learned later that Gershon's quietness came from a deep feeling of low self-esteem and an inferiority complex. He was silent because his self-esteem was so low he believed he had nothing worthwhile to say. Many factors can cause a man to lose confidence in himself so that he loses the ability to guide his own life, to live independently, to love. In this case, the cause was his mother, Hodel.

I discovered later, to my deep sorrow, that his mother's vicious, domineering, and overbearing personality left him an empty shell. By the time he was a young adult, Gershon had nothing left to say. His ambition, confidence, intellectual energy and personality were destroyed by his mother long before I appeared. She did everything physically possible for him and his brother, Shlomo. Whenever they tried to express an opinion, she shut them up with her favorite expression, "I know everything; you know nothing." They believed her.

Gershon chauffeured people in his car because his mother used him to drive her friends to meetings and shopping. I came to believe that she employed his driving to "buy" false friends whose flattery fed her needs.

During the weeks we dated, like many another naive person, I thought I could change him. I started to ask his opinions about various things, but he always answered, "I don't know." I must have deluded myself to continue accepting his dating invitations, but he had such a sad face, pathetic enough to arouse pity in anyone with half a heart, that I couldn't make him sadder by refusing his dates. And I thought I could make him happy.

One eventful night, Gershon asked me to marry him. He said he loved me. I thought I could change him because he was, I believed, such a good person. Believe me when I tell you one basic truth: you can not change another person. You can only change yourself. **YOU GET WHAT YOU SEE.**

Out of pity, out of delusion, I said yes. I never realized what I was getting into; I never understood for one minute that I was dealing with a very ill person. Even when, as a *kallah*, I began to notice strange things about him, such as a far-off glassy look in his eyes and weird, long silences, I went along with everything he said. Love was truly blind, and deaf as well.

Later in my marriage, I realized that engaged people must acknowledge and recognize clues that appear strange and odd. That is when I really came to understand deeply that one person cannot change another. I wanted to shout to every young girl and boy, **NEVER** enter a marriage based on the notion that you can change your spouse's habits. **NEVER** marry out of pity believing you can repair a broken person. What you see is what you get!

Teach your children that. Mine already know.

Chapter Two:Mamale

Shortly after Gershon proposed, he invited me to meet his mother, Hodel, whom he called "Mamele". We drove out to her apartment.

As we entered, I was shocked to find myself in a depressing, dirty atmosphere. My future mother-in-law, in an award winning performance, portrayed herself as a simple woman, lonely and ignorant. Thus Hodel concealed her true nature right from the very beginning.

I learned slowly and sadly that she was a domineering, sly woman, jealous and selfishly cruel. She used passive aggressiveness, emotional blackmail, even brainwashing, to get what she wanted from her helpless, hapless sons, and from everyone else. She destroyed Gershon and his brother Shlomo; she tried to destroy me as well.

Remember that the commandment "honor your mother" does not grant the mother the right to rule her adult children, to dominate them, or to manipulate their lives. But Hodel's manipulation was habitual. She constantly talked about herself, how beautiful she had been, what a wonderful homemaker she was, while subtly knocking her friends and speaking ill of them. While preparing this book compels me to speak candidly of her, I have concealed both my true identity and Hodel's. I did this to preserve privacy and to avoid *loshen hora*, which I despise, and which marred every conversation with her.

As we visited, while she was serving and talking, I noticed without analyzing it, that she buttered my fiancé's bread, but not his brother's. I had never seen this kind of behavior before, not for an adult son, but I was to see plenty of it in the future.

Hodel lived in the past. Little did I know that Gershon's silent depression was due to being raised in an unhealthy environment where Mamale constantly put him down on one hand and treated him like a boyfriend on the other, using him and his brother to fill her emotional void. Later in my marriage, I realized that this unhealthy relationship had a name and a prototype: the classic Oedipus Complex.

From our first meeting, Hodel spoke with longing of her late husband, Mendel, a timid man she had nursed, she would say, "better than a mother" through his final illness. Mendel, she said, always told her how delicious her food was. She said she loved to ask him if it was better than his mother's cooking and, of course, he would say that it was. To Hodel, this was a supreme compliment. And when Mendel died (since Shlomo was married and Gershon was single and still living at home), she turned to Gershon as a replacement for him as the man in her life.

I came to understand this, and to shudder at how abnormal it was, but in my mind I clung to the belief that I could rescue Gershon, and change him. I did not realize the extent of his illness. He was totally beyond any help, even if he had wanted it. If I had understood what I was seeing on that pre-marital visit, I could have refused to marry Gershon and my life would have been radically different. But I did not see, and I was already engaged. It is hard for young girls to understand that a broken engagement is a minor event compared to a life in a bad marriage or a broken one.

As I got to know Hodel, I began to perceive her as a vicious woman, a woman who did not care if she destroyed her sons mentally, physically and emotionally. Once, she admitted feeling terrible guilt over ruining Shlomo's marriage to Lana, a beautiful girl with whom he had two children, Abraham and Yaacov. But Hodel's words of sincere regret were forgotten as quickly as they were uttered, because her destructive, passive aggressive behavior never altered despite her expression of guilt. She buried her regrets instantly. I wonder if she ever really felt guilty at all; it wasn't in her character.

In many discussions, if Hodel felt she was losing ground, she would simply faint. A doctor would be summoned. Everyone would make a great fuss. Her friends would all be told she was ill and they would troop in to visit, bringing food and pity. When we were just newlyweds the doctor told us she was faking, but Gershon would still sit beside her bed and just stare at her oblivious to the world.

I tried not to see his glassy eyes, his restless twitchy body, but my observations never really mattered. He would not leave her side. Even though she managed to read *The Jewish Forward* and to coerce him to prepare whatever food she developed a craving for, he remained gullible. She convinced him that he could not leave her side. Baby-sitting his Mamale cost Gershon time from his business, but he felt it was his job to nurse her and he persisted.

Meanwhile, Shlomo ignored her, healthy or not. But, after he left Lana, he lived with his mother. Every night he had the same routine: he came home from work, ate the supper Hodel prepared, lit his pipe, sat in his chair and read his paper. He might as well have been a piece of furniture.

Hodel was dumbfounded when people asked her why she took in her married son, a self-sufficient adult. She also could not understand when her friends wanted to spend some holiday time at home with their families and not at a hotel with her. She was extremely upset that she did not come first in their plans.

I spent much of my time during my marriage trying to figure Hodel out, because she had such an enormous, negative impact on my life. Most marriages involve two people, which is as it should be. My marriage had three participants: myself, Gershon and Hodel. She had treated her meek husband Mendel as a son and her grown sons as husbands; she treated me only as an intruder. She manipulated the men in her life as much out of habit as out of any specific motive, and she poisoned everyone who came into contact with her.

I first began to understand what she was doing to her son and to me the morning after our wedding.

The wedding itself was beautiful. We held it in New York City and it was so lovely I've even wondered if I somehow attracted the *evil eye*, because everything that followed was so ugly.

On our wedding night, Gershon was totally unable to consummate our marriage. The next morning, I was awakened by the shrill ring of the telephone. Mamale wanted to ask Gershon what I had prepared for him for breakfast. He blushed and lowered his head.

I had a dreadful, literally filled with dread, sense of intrusion, which made me very uncomfortable on top of my youthful bewilderment at his nighttime failure. I also didn't understand his reaction to her call. He got increasingly agitated as they talked. He became jittery and made peculiar body manifestations. He got very nervous. He would take the phone from his ear, twirl it around several times as Hodel kept talking, and with his free hand, he'd touch his hair, ears, and eyes. He then returned to the conversation. I couldn't figure it out, but I was to see it again and again. He would not discuss it, or much of anything else.

I realized I had to get him to talk to me, but I failed. Even when we were with friends, he would clam up. In groups, he spoke only to very old men and at home spent his time sitting at the kitchen table with a Bible in front of him. I don't think he studied anything, but his supposed scholarly concentration worked well as a ploy for avoiding conversation.

Gershon could not consummate our marriage for several weeks. He managed it only after finally taking medication. I knew I had to be patient and wait for the medication to work. According to Jewish law, two people can only live together for a certain length of time without consummating their marriage. If the marriage isn't consummated by then, the woman automatically receives a "*get*" (religious proclamation of divorce). A "*get*" based on sexual failure would have embarrassed Gershon and followed him for the rest of his life.

But Gershon didn't just have a sexual problem; he was a cold individual who didn't seem to need affection or know how to show affection. After a few weeks, when we began to have marital relations, I hoped that our improved physical relationship would generate a closer personal rapport.

Meanwhile, I continued my office job and traveled on the subway from Manhattan to Brooklyn. I came home to cook and clean, but I began to notice to my considerable dismay that Gershon, like his mother, was not concerned with personal cleanliness.

Being a "*mitzvah girl*", every Sunday, without fail, I innocently asked Hodel to join us at whatever we were doing. She always accepted. I feel now that she was craftily seizing every opportunity to put her destructive schemes to work, but such a thing would never have crossed my mind as a new bride. I also learned later that I was wrong to invite her to join us weekly. I know now that young couples need to spend their leisure time together, just the two of them, alone, getting to know each other.

Today I see that I would have been far better off, and so would Gershon, if we had moved his mother away from us and I hadn't been so accepting of her. There was a lovely senior citizen home in Long Beach where she would have been with her friends and done as she pleased, from wearing the dreadful clothes she loved, to complaining to her heart's content.

Years later, I suggested it to Gershon and he rejected the idea. He felt that if he asked his mother to move into a senior citizens' home, she would think she was dying, so he wasn't going to do that to her. It was the wrong decision. If Hodel had moved, she would have been far happier. She could have had constant activity and companionship plus maid service, doctors and nurses at hand, and three meals a day served in a beautiful dining room. Instead, she lived in her grimy, lonely apartment with no friends and nothing to do all day except make trouble. She made plenty of that, busily pushing people one against another in her quiet way. I made the mistake of giving her the key to our apartment, a privilege which she abused. I never had any privacy. Hodel made her own life bitter, not just mine and Gershon's. Even people who did things for her received insults and criticism. Hodel generally did not seem to like the company of women, and Gershon shied away from men.

My husband danced attendance to her, no matter how unkindly she treated him. In the mornings, Gershon got up and rushed to the synagogue, always saying that he had no time to do anything for me, such as taking out the trash. "I can't do it," he would say. Yet, he made time to do things for his mother. He would shop for her, visit her, deliver her newspaper and a quart of milk, catering to her every whim. Many mornings, it was ten o'clock before he came home, interrupted whatever I was doing, and asked me to serve him breakfast. When I was working, he took what he wanted from the kitchen, but always left the dishes on the table for me.

It was usually around eleven a.m. when Gershon first started his workday but not until he had made another stop at his mother's. They spoke on the phone several times a day, like lovers, although he never called me, even after we had children. At five p.m., Gershon would return to his mother, then go to synagogue for evening prayers, then come to our apartment around eight p.m. for dinner, and then go back again to his mother until eleven or twelve p.m., which later turned out to be a blessing in disguise.

Even in my youthful naiveté, it didn't take me long to

realize that I had stumbled into a very strange situation. I rode the subway to work every day and was gone between eight a.m. and six p.m. I was often wiped out in the evenings. I fixed up our apartment beautifully, more for me than for him, because I was accustomed to cleanliness and pleasantness. He was raised in dirt and ugliness. Hodel came over one evening, when I was particularly exhausted, and made a big deal about wanting to know what I was cooking for her son. Today, I wonder why I never thought to purchase cooked foods. I managed to put a stop to such visits, but I could never break his routine of visiting her morning, evening and night.

She was the third person in a relationship designed for two.

Chapter Three: Our Son

About a month after Gershon started taking his medicine we began to have normal sexual relations. Approximately three months after we got married, I had an attack of dizziness and nausea as I climbed the subway stairs on my way to work. I went home. Gershon was still there, and I told him, "I don't feel well." "You don't look well," he answered, and walked out to go to his mother's apartment. As he closed the door, I regarded him with new bitterness: if I had been his mother, he would have told me to go to bed and then he would have carried in a chair to sit beside me. Instead, I was alone, but not for long. Shortly thereafter I went to the doctor's office and discovered, miraculously, that I was pregnant. I was joyful at the news, and have found in my son Dovid, a source of joy since that moment.

However, I soon discovered that my husband understood nothing about the hormonal changes a woman undergoes during pregnancy. He was unaware of my need for emotional support, and both unwilling and unable to offer any. Gradually, I realized that his emotions were frozen. He had no feelings about anything except his mother. The only emotional actions he could muster were attempts to gain his mother's pity, and this was all she had to offer in the form of warmth.

I worked until my seventh month of pregnancy, which fell on the *Succos* holiday. Gershon wanted to spend the *Succos* week at a hotel with his mother, so they picked me up at lunchtime at my office on Wall Street to drive to the hotel. Hodel began to eat the sandwich she had made for herself. I was famished, but she had made nothing for me to eat. When we stopped at a service station, Gershon told me, "Go inside and buy a chocolate bar." "You know I can't have chocolate," I told him, dismayed and queasy, but it made no impression. He didn't care if I was pregnant, if I became ill or if I felt neglected. I was the third party, the intruder on that voyage. Sitting in the car, I made a decision: I would not allow my child to get too close to it's father. I would protect my baby.

During the nine months of pregnancy, a young couple often becomes closer, drawn together by the joy and anticipation, by hopes and dreams for their child. But I was married to a cold, unfeeling man, so I never experienced the beauty of such bonding within a loving relationship. Hodel came to our apartment every evening during those months, and I allowed it. Gershon would walk her home. When they left, I always wondered what destructive things she was saying about me as they strolled.

Today, husbands participate in the delivery of their children, witnessing their wives' labor pains and thus growing in empathy. I don't believe Gershon could have handled that without a physical breakdown and a fit of twitches and weird gestures. The only responsibility he could manage was catering to his mother.

My labor lasted twelve hours. My son was a breach baby and labor was a lonely nightmare, but my wonderful doctor was able to turn my son's head into the proper position for a normal birth. I was finally put into a deep sleep for the delivery and awoke to the beautiful words, "*mazel tov, mazel tov*, it's a boy."

I had left an immaculate apartment when I went to the hospital. I returned not to a joyful welcome, but to a pigsty, even though Gershon could have easily afforded to bring in a maid to clean up after himself. Looking at the wreckage he had created, I reconfirmed my opinion that he had no self-esteem or self-respect at all. *Torah* deems cleanliness important for a person, but someone raised otherwise is more comfortable dirty than clean. I handed my baby over to the nurse we had temporarily engaged and got busy cleaning up my home.

Our newborn son, whom we named Dovid, brought me great joy, but he didn't seem to hold his father's attention at all. Gershon's schedule never varied: eight a.m. synagogue; ten a.m. Mamale; eleven a.m. home for breakfast; a workday punctuated by calls to Hodel but not to me or his son; five p.m. visit Mamale, six p.m. synagogue, seven p.m. Mamale, eight p.m. home for supper, and then one last visit to his mother before bed. Later on it turned out that Gershon's lack of attention for our little boy was a blessing in disguise, but during Dovid's babyhood his father's distance was not in my control. I just handled it as well as I could.

Soon after the baby came, my mother-in-law decided she wanted to spend the summer at a bungalow colony in the country. Thinking I was doing a *mitzvah*, I agreed to go with her when she asked me. I realized she was afraid to go alone and all I feared was boredom. Being a city girl, I hate the country in all forms, especially bungalow colonies. I accompanied her and enjoyed having my little son with me. But, I was bored.

One Saturday night, the bungalow colony staged a third-rate stage show. Hodel insisted that I go to the show with Gershon, who had joined us for a few days. She said she would take care of the baby. The offer was rare, so I took her up on it. But as we sat through the show, a rare "date," Gershon suddenly turned to me and said, "I wish Mamale was here." I took the opportunity to leave the show and go back to the cabin to tell Hodel that her son missed her. She dressed quickly and ran to join him. I think I did a *mitzvah* that night, and I don't regret it, but it made my situation clear to me. These were abnormal people caught in the cycle of a deepening, dangerous dependency. Later on, I felt *Hashem* reimbursed me in full for the good deeds I did in that marriage, not that you do a *mitzvah* to get reimbursed, but sometimes that's the way it works. But first, as often happens, things got worse before they got better.

Chapter Four: A Daughter and Some Doubts

I was living with a man who was full of surprises. One night, he came home and told me, he didn't ask me, he told me, that his mother was moving in next door to us because she wanted to be closer to him. This situation was so clearly out of my hands that I just continued calmly reading my book, outwardly detached, inwardly burning, as he filled me in on their plans.

A couple of days later, Hodel called me and asked me to come help her pack and clean up her old apartment. "Of course," I said. Another *mitzvah*. I can't describe the filth and mess I dealt with in that apartment. When the day was over, no one thanked me, but by then I didn't really expect it. I told them I was going to stop some place and get something to eat. "Don't you have anything left over from *Shabbos* that you can eat?" Gershon asked. I couldn't even answer him; I just walked out. I wondered what kind of a husband lets his wife do hard physical labor all afternoon for his mother and then doesn't even offer to take her out for dinner. But then I answered my own question; he was, at least, consistent. He could not see beyond his mother. It was totally out of my control. It was, in his sickness, even out of his control. I chalked it up to another *mitzvah*.

Needless to say, when Hodel moved in next door, I gave her a key to our home. I never had another minute of peace or privacy. Our quiet house was suddenly a public arena.

Because their grandmother now spent her days at my apartment, Shlomo's two sons also kept coming in and out. The family never knocked, they just assumed they could come in at any time. I became close to my nephews, and I will tell you about them shortly. Although they disappointed me eventually, I think I represented the only real parental love they ever received. There was never at any time a thank you.

Another mother-in-law might have told her friends that her daughter-in-law made a lovely home, took care of her grandchildren beautifully, and welcomed her into her home, but instead Hodel found destructive things to tell my neighbors. Before her arrival, all of us in my apartment building had gotten along fine. But she was a master of vicious insinuations and she instigated conflict. Soon my neighbors were at odds with each other. Why did she spread insults? Why did she foster dissension? For reasons I can't fathom to this day, I think she was determined to destroy our marriage just as she ruined Shlomo's marriage. After she spent any length of time away from our apartment, she pumped my husband to tell her everything that had happened in her absence. And he complied. He told her all our private goings on, and they became grist for her mill.

Yet amidst this negativity and chaos, I persuaded Gershon to go back on the medication which made it possible for us to have physical relations again. It took effect and I was rewarded with a second pregnancy. Again, I found labor dreadful and painful, but I gave birth to our angel of a daughter, Avigail. Again, the sounds of *mazel tov* rang in my ears.

Again, I came home from the hospital to a filthy, dirty house and a very long recuperation. I was overjoyed to be back with Dovid because I had feared Hodel and Gershon would neglect him in my absence, as they did. Luckily, I had the same nurse I had engaged before, to take care of me and the baby, so I tried to give my son some love and attention. Little Avigail was a good and beautiful baby, and a great joy to Dovid and to me.

Gershon continued to keep his distance. He just didn't know what to do when he was around children, and his mother's reactions confused him all the more and fed his increasing alienation.

Hodel was extremely uncomfortable when I kissed, hugged and openly loved my children. She told her son it was some kind of strange behavior on my part. Fortunately, he was foolish enough to tell me every vicious thing she said.

From time to time, I began to think that I had to get out of there, even with a small boy and an infant daughter. **I knew I was in an uncontrollable situation, so I controlled the things I could.** This is extremely important and I offer it to you as a critical piece of advice: **manage what you can manage**.

I made the best of my bad situation by keeping myself immaculate and beautiful, dressing myself and my children well, and keeping our house spotless and pretty. I took in help when I needed it. I made lots of friends and opened our home often as a central place for people to congregate amid warm hospitality. On *Shabbos*, our home was lively with my friends and, later, my children's friends. I love people and, by then, I couldn't stand to spend a minute alone with Gershon. He and I hardly ever spoke anymore except to argue, which was instigated by Mamale. Even though money was never any object, thank G-d, he began to complain frequently that he couldn't afford one thing or another. I ignored him. I wasn't going to change my life style because his mother kept him home until noon. However, he got plenty of commiseration from her when he complained about my spending. This did not stop her when she decided to spend money on herself. In fact he would take her shopping and waste a whole business day.

He also doled out inappropriate charity (I never objected to genuine tzedukah) to people who simply didn't believe in working, including to some who lived in million dollar homes. But giving inappropriate charity would have been a minor fault in a loving, caring husband; in a misanthropic cold fish, it was just one more burden to bear.

The less I looked at his depressed, frowning face, the better I felt. In general, I managed to be happy, especially when I was around my two children, who were growing nicely. They barely knew their father. Sadly, that turned out to be just as well.

Chapter Five: Learning to Cope

I was maturing as I raised my children in this atmosphere. Some of my ideas and convictions began to crystallize. I discovered that when things are beyond your control, you need to take a constructive, positive attitude. Do not change your basic values or your lifestyle. Bide your time. Learn, if you can, to willingly let go of things you cannot control. Have faith. Everything is *bashert*. It's not worth making yourself ill. Life is beautiful and is meant to be lived. Find the beauty where you can.

I am just describing a few incidents out of thousands that I have experienced. I do not intend to complain, but to give you an intimate picture of what I went through in confronting my husband's illness and how I handled it. Nothing should be allowed to rob you of your spirit. Your main goal, until you can change your bad situation, or leave it, is to keep yourself and your children happy and well, mentally and physically.

If you are with a husband who has a dangerous or uncontrollable temper, you must develop strategies for coping and for sheltering your children, until the day comes when you can leave. I am fortunate in only one instance: Gershon was never physically violent. He never struck me or threatened my physical safety or our children's. If he had, my slow departure would have become an instant departure. You are not permitted to endanger your children; you are entitled to physical safety and a life without violence. If your husband loses his temper, but it doesn't get physical, you might be able to weather the storm. You can explain to your children that *Abba* is not well and needs special attention or help. But if he gets violent, recognize that you and your children may be in danger. You may want to leave with your children, so be sure to call the police to obtain a restraining order. You must remain calm and reassure your children. Try not to upset them anymore than necessary. They need to feel secure. It's all up to you.

The tools I found most useful were the ability to make a decision and the ability to decide to ignore something, and then to ignore it successfully. When something occurred, I would stop for a moment and ask myself, "Am I in control of this situation or is this situation beyond my control?" If I found that I could answer "Yes, I'm in control," I would attempt to set limits defining what I wanted, expected, and could achieve. Often I couldn't set limits until events occurred where lines had to be drawn. A few examples:

One morning I was feeding Dovid and heard a key turn in the lock. Hodel entered without knocking and told me to stop feeding the baby. She wanted me to go to her apartment, get the company books and give her the account balance so she could report it to her son who was on the phone. I calmly told her I would not stop feeding the baby, but that she could bring me the books and I would look up the balance. I was upset at her lack of maternal feelings and at her constant "business first before anything" attitude, but I would not fall into her trap. If I had gotten excited or refused her with anger, the result would have been a three hundred pound woman falling on my bedroom floor in a fake faint, and her son would end up spending a great deal of time staring at her in bed, catering to her every whim and losing time from the business. I had no intention of beginning that cycle or of trying to pick her up off the floor. After she had come and gone with the books, I called my brother-in-law and told him not to send her to me on a business errand again. The whole time, I never stopped feeding the baby. For this one round, at least, I was in control.

Hodel was not an organized housekeeper and she often ran out of necessities. One morning, I went to my refrigerator to prepare some scrambled eggs for my son, and there were no eggs. I counted to ten and went next door to find Mamale preparing my eggs. She said she had run out of eggs, but she had never asked me if it was alright to take mine. I explained that she had taken food intended for the baby and that she mustn't ever take things without asking again. Both her sons got mad at me and defended her, but she knew what was going on. She never did it again.

Sometimes the value in a difficult situation is that it waves a red flag and alerts you to the fact that you are going to have to make a change, as hard as taking such action might be.

Some of the incidents I experienced had a comical side and this one seemed to at first, but it proved to me that my husband and his mother could no longer be left alone with Dovid and Avigail.

My mother-in-law offered to show me her special fish recipe. She often came up with such schemes which looked like favors on the surface, but actually provided her with time in her son's home, opportunities to spy, and a chance to display her "superior" skills. I figured it was a *mitzvah* to take her up on her offer. After all, she was lonely and what harm could come of it, other than having her pillage my groceries and wreck my kitchen. After doing just that, she finally put the fish on the burner to cook. I cleaned up the kitchen and carried the garbage to the incinerator only to return to a kitchen full of billowing black smoke. Hodel had never lowered the gas or checked on her famous dish. My whole apartment was thick with the smoke of the burning fish and my two children were asleep in the bedroom.

Gershon was oblivious to the whole thing. He said he didn't see any smoke, he was busy watching television. But I saw it and quickly ran to the children's room to check on them; they were sleeping soundly and the smoke had not penetrated to their bedroom, thank G-d. I went back to the kitchen and handed Hodel the burnt pot. I think she would have cheerfully loved to pin the whole thing on me so she could tell the neighbors a juicy story, but she was not nearly as eager to say, "My son was so preoccupied watching T.V. that his apartment filled up with black smoke and the smell of burning fish, and he never noticed."

After I had cleaned up the kitchen and thrown open the windows to clear the stench of fish out of the air, I finally made a very difficult and serious decision: my children could never be allowed to be left totally alone with their father. He was too oblivious and not dependable. No more unsupervised walks, no pizza excursions unless I came along. I started to think seriously again about making an exodus, not only for my children's sake, but for mine too.

The children were getting older, they would soon catch on. It would be impossible for them not to recognize their father's instability for much longer.

Chapter 6: The Jewish Holidays

Y ou would think that being *Torah* observant Jews would have been helpful to me and my children. It is true that faith was critical to our survival. But in our household, every *yontif* was a battleground and a separate learning experience. Our beautiful Jewish holidays shape our lives and can add richness and joy if personal trauma doesn't mar them. The Jewish calendar offers opportunities to appreciate *Hashem* and to celebrate year round. Each holiday has its traditions and customs, its inner meaning and its obligations and events.

Here are just a few holiday glimpses so that you can understand the life I was leading, the true profile of emotional abuse.

Shavuos

Celebrating the arrival of summer and the end of the counting of the *omer, Shavuos* is a beautiful *yontif*. I remember the *erev Shavuos* when my mother-in-law came to my apartment complaining that it was a half-hour before *yontif* and my husband had not yet brought her any flowers. She spoke in the words and tones of someone complaining about a negligent boyfriend.

"Where is he now?" she asked querulously. "He always buys me flowers."

He came in a few minutes later with a bunch of dead flowers. His mother preened and dimpled like a girl as he, first, handed her a bunch. She smiled broadly from cheek to cheek. He then gave me a cluster. I thanked him and went into the kitchen, where I threw the poor wilted things away. I later took a few flowers from my girlfriend. I give Gershon credit for feebly trying to mark the holiday, but I resented the half-hearted result. He never knew or cared. His mother was happy, and that seemed to be enough.

A couple of years later, on the night of *Shavuos,* I heard a loud banging on my door. Gershon was not home, and when I opened the door, my neighbor yelled that our building was on fire. I quickly picked up my daughter from her crib, put shoes on my son, and walked out into a hallway full of smoke. People were running and coughing, like a scene from a disaster movie. We had to use the stairs to leave the building, but we were glad to emerge into the fresh air. When we came out, I saw my husband standing and chatting, totally unconcerned that his wife and children had been inside a burning building. One of my friends invited us to come into her nearby apartment until the all clear signal was sounded. When the smoke cleared, the fire had been contained to one apartment, and no major damage was done. Gershon had no way of knowing that would be the outcome.

The children and I went home and found him sitting, learning and eating; he was completely unconcerned. Yet one of his favorite stories was of the time that his mother had phoned him in New York, when there was a fire in the mountains, and he had jumped into his car and hurried up to the bungalow colony to be sure she was safe.

Purim

In the early days of my marriage, when my children were very little, *yontif* dinners for the family were always held at my home, including the *Purim seudah.* The *megillah* was also read in my house.

As friction grew between me and Hodel, it became

impossible to continue that pattern. At *Purim*, every man, woman and child is commanded to listen to the reading of the *megillah*, the beautiful story of Queen Esther and the survival of the Jewish people. If a woman is unable to go to *shul* to hear the reading, the *megillah* is traditionally read for her at home. One year I had invited some of our friends to share the *Purim seudah* with us, but as the time drew near to read the *megillah*, Gershon got visibly nervous. Finally he stood up and said he was going next door to read the *megillah* for his mother and that I could listen in on the phone. I was appalled, but I complied to avoid an argument because of the special company we had joining us. I did not want to further dampen the festivities. The following year, Gershon's cousins joined us for the *seudah*, and he suggested doing the same thing again. This time, I refused. I calmly stated that I wanted him to read the *megillah* at our table and I suggested that, this time, Hodel could call up and listen on the phone. Instead, Gershon went to his mother's house to read it and then read it again in our home. What kind of a mother would force her son to read the *megillah* twice, knowing what a difficult task it is?

Tisha B'Av

I discovered early on that Gershon's mother taught her sons that she came first. Hodel and I were in the mountains the summer Dovid was an infant and I spent the fast day of *Tisha B'Av* with her. After the fast, she said, "Why hasn't Gerson phoned? My son always calls to find out how I am after a fast."

I realized then that my situation was beyond help. He did finally call her and he wasn't interested in anyone else, not his wife or his children.

✡✡✡

Throughout the cycle of holidays each year of my marriage, I tried to make the *yom tovim* special and meaningful. I still wonder what happened to the invincible tradition of the staunch Orthodox family, so unified, that even *Bilaam* who was supposed to curse us, blessed us instead. Family unity is exactly what I wanted but I could never have it, not with my sick husband. Unity has to be the goal of everyone in a family, not just one person fighting against the odds.

Chapter Seven: The Nephews

When I first met my divorced brother-in-law's sons, Abraham and Yaacov, they were ages six and ten. They lived in emotional turmoil. Their father, Shlomo, paid them scant attention. He would glance up from his newspaper, offer them a word of praise or encouragement, and then return to his reading without really pausing for them. Meanwhile, Hodel constantly spewed insults about their mother Lana, who remained in her own expense-paid apartment, eating out nightly, not working, having everything bought for her by her husband. Despite his mother's insinuations, Shlomo jumped to do Lana's bidding, even to the extent of running out in the evening to bring her a New York Times newspaper.

Lana could not look after the boys, so they "lived with" their father, who carried out no real responsibilities on their behalf. Even Hodel, who supposedly cooked and cleaned for the three of them, asked nothing of Shlomo. Actually, Hodel was paid to cook for them, but they always ate in my house.

Hodel never asked Shlomo to help her or do anything in particular for his sons. In fact, she once got very angry when she learned that he had helped Lana with household chores after work. The one exception I remember was the night Hodel asked Shlomo to clean out the bathroom. He complained bitterly about how tired he was but she let it pass, and he continued to clean.

Abraham and Yaacov spent most *Shabbosim* with us, although they slept on Hodel's couch while their father slept in her bedroom with her (which I felt was obviously problematic). My nephews had the key to our apartment, which became their second home. They ate their meals at our table and discussed all their problems with me. Yaacov even spent two weeks with me in the mountains each year, before he began going to camp. I was never thanked or offered a penny in reimbursement, not that I was looking for it or would have taken it. I do my good deeds from the heart without demanding anything in return.

I pitied my nephews as I became a surrogate mother to them, a *mitzvah* I never regretted. They were children in my home and that made them my responsibility. It wasn't their fault that they could not depend upon the other adults in their lives. I would bustle about feeding them and trying to entertain them and listen to their little concerns. I took them wherever I took my kids.

My nephews had the key to our apartment, until one night when I went into my kitchen to get Avigail her bottle. I became very frightened at seeing the silhouette of a man standing in the shadows in my living room. It turned out to be Yaacov who had come in unexpectedly, and was standing in the dark. When I regained my composure, I asked for his key and firmly established the policy that no one, not even he, should enter my home without knocking and asking me first.

Even though I requested advance notice, and usually got it, my nephews were always welcome in my home. They never stopped coming, even though they had a mother, maternal grandparents and maternal cousins, uncles, aunts and other extended family, not to mention their father and Mamale. No one seemed to bother with them except me, even to the point of inviting them for a *Shabbos* or *yom tov*. I suppose they felt love and security in my house, yet they never thanked me in any way, as good manners would dictate. They just weren't raised to do it.

I tried to do what I could for those boys, but Dovid and Avigail were always my priority. One *Shavuos*, I became aware that Yaacov was beginning to manifest the deep emotional problems that I thought were inevitable based upon his upbringing and his lack of parental love. My children and I were preparing to go out for a walk (my husband slept when we went so that he would have the energy later to walk with his mother), when Yaacov ran into our apartment from Hodel's unit next door, grabbed a box of *matzo* off our dining table, threw it all over the apartment, and ran out. Hoping against experience that my husband would clean up his nephew's mess when he woke up, I decided not to deprive Dovid and Avigail of their outing. We took our walk. Of course, when we returned, the mess was still there. Gershon was sitting at the table eating an orange, and the floor around him was still covered with pieces of *matzo*. I told my kids, "We have a fun game to play, but first let's pick up the *matzo*." That is when they began to resent their cousins.

They were astounded, and so was I, when I took the refilled box of *matzo* they had gathered, walked next door to Hodel's apartment, and threw the crumbs and pieces all over her rug and furniture. Then my kids and I went out together again.

I don't pretend to you that this was the best behavior on my part, but Hodel and Shlomo had to be forced to pay attention to these boys and to curb their destructive tendencies. Perhaps they needed the object lesson and I needed the outlet. I admit it was satisfying, if childish, to take the mess next door.

As it later happened, Abraham and Yaacov were very destructive in their behavior toward my children. Once the children and I moved to Florida, the boys and Shlomo never contacted us or expressed any interest in their cousins. Not once in all those years did they concern themselves with our welfare.

Today, when I think about Abraham and Yaacov, I realize that their childhood passed without true familial love, except from me, their aunt. If their father and grandmother and uncle did not respect and value my contribution to them, how could these children value me, or themselves?

Chapter Eight: More Mamale and Other Last Straws

I am trying very hard not to make this volume a long diatribe against my mother-in-law. I do feel however that the emotional abuse in my marriage stemmed from her behavior, and from the demands she placed upon her son. He too was an instrument of abuse, but in many ways he was her instrument against me. He became so weak-willed and so emotionally disturbed, he was simply her tool. A few examples:

All my life, I felt that *Hashem* was always by my side guiding me, but during the following incident, He worked overtime on my behalf. I have always loved to save, spend, and enjoy my money, but not to blow it on silly non-gratifying things. I have the knack of saving money; by nature, I'm a careful and frugal shopper and I have luckily been able to pass this quality along to my children. When my children saved up their nickels and dimes, I always patted them on the back and told them what a great effort they had made.

When Gershon and I were newlyweds, we set up a joint bank account. I depended upon the trust that is supposed to exist between a husband and wife. With my salary and my careful management of the household budget, I was able to accumulate a good amount of money.

Early in our marriage, I thought Hodel was my friend. When she asked me personal questions, I answered her freely, not suspecting she would use what I said against me. At that point, I did not realize that she totally lacked common sense, but in the long run it was a blessing in disguise. She asked me how much money I had in the bank and I told her. She promptly told Gershon to take the money away from me, hoping, I guess, that if I were penniless, I would be more dependent upon her and would kowtow to her. Behind my back, Gershon withdrew two thousand dollars of my careful savings from the bank. He never mentioned it to me. The next time I went to make a deposit, I almost dropped my baby I was so astounded and upset. I struggled to remain calm and in control in front of the teller and quietly asked her if I could open a separate account for my children, with myself as trustee. When she assured me that I could, I transferred the small amount left in our joint account into a new, separate account. Then I borrowed a pair of scissors from her and cut my old bank book in half.

When I served Gershon dinner that night, I dropped the two halves of the bank book on the table in front of him. I didn't yell, shout accusations or waste time and energy destructively. I offered no angry words and tendered no explanations. Years later, I got the two thousand dollars back because I started a *din torah* against him, but he refused to pay the twenty one years of interest which I lost and refused to pay me nine years of moral involvement.

The old bank book had been my ticket to Florida, to the exodus I had begun to plan for myself and my children. Thank goodness, Gershon and Hodel acted so rashly that I caught them in time to understand I needed to establish a separate account. This way, I was able to plan our departure in style and privacy. I never discussed it with anyone. No one knew my business. I could continue to instill in my children the emotional, physical and mental stability they needed. The one warning I offer to all wives, especially in situations where any type of abuse has occurred, is insist on your own checking and saving account **in your own name**. Money is essential for independence.

Gershon told me one morning that his mother had decided that he needed a vacation from his domestic responsibilities (which he never fulfilled anyway), so he decided to go away for *Shabbos* with another couple, leaving the children home with me. I asked him only to tell the kids that he had to be away on business, so they wouldn't feel he was neglecting them. He had no idea what I was talking about. I didn't scream, lecture or fight. His sickness was becoming more apparent to me daily and I felt a little relieved at the idea of having him gone for a *Shabbos*.

One cold winter, I went briefly to Florida with the children and during that trip I received a surprise phone call from Gershon. He told me that he was going to Europe on business, although I knew he never went three feet away from his mother. I was having a good time and, candidly, didn't give his travels a second thought until I got home and my neighbors told me that he had gone to Israel with his mother. My only thought was why Hodel hadn't taken Shlomo as well, since she had already ruined his marriage. And now, she was succeeding in ruining mine.

The following January and February brought bitter winter weather and the children caught persistent colds. They were out of school more than they were in, so I decided to take them back to Florida to recuperate for a couple of weeks.

While I was away, my mother-in-law had my beautiful apartment, which I had painstakingly decorated, coordinating everything around colors I like, repainted in her awful taste. What could I do when I returned? I ripped some of the tacky paper off my beautiful shelves and took the kids out for a pizza. This was now out of my control. On the way back, I picked up a few boxes. In the back of my mind, I had had enough and I was getting ready to pack up and leave. I wasn't completely ready yet, but I was getting there. The camel's back needed a few more straws broken. I was accustomed to having Hodel come between me and my husband, but she now began to come between him and our children, no matter how hard I had tried to maintain an illusion of unity for their sake.

Every now and then, I asked my husband, who is fluent in Hebrew, to stay home for an evening and help Dovid with his tons of Hebrew language homework.

One evening, as my son and his father were studying, a terrible banging on the door startled all of us. My husband ran to the door and encountered his infuriated mother, who insisted that he had to take her to meeting. Completely forgetting our son and their work together, he ran to the coat closet for his hat and coat, and drove her and her friends to their meeting. I tried to help Dovid with his work, but more importantly I tried to console him. I finally assured him that the very next day, I would engage a tutor to help him continue to be the smart, hard-working little boy he was. When I finally got him settled that night, I reflected on Hodel's selfish stubbornness. I am sure it never crossed her mind to wonder what family activity she might be interrupting when she pounded on our door.

In a larger sense, by refusing to seek activity and friendship among people her own age, Hodel was missing out on a great deal of enjoyment and she was deliberately becoming a burden to her son and his family. How much richer her life would have been if she could have taken advantage of the many opportunities senior citizens have for entertainment, trips and leisure fun. Her main activities involved having my husband chauffeur her to meetings and stores.

If we had an open evening, she would be in her house and my husband would sit with her. But if she found out that we had plans, she always thought of something, some way, to interrupt.

She also made herself comfortable with my belongings. Hodel told me, once, that when I wasn't home she went through my dresser drawers. When my engagement ring was missing from its usual spot in my top drawer, I knew what had happened. Gershon timidly confirmed my suspicions. Without permission, his mother had entered my bedroom, rifled through my bureau, taken my ring and locked it away in her safe deposit box. The safe deposit box did not have my name on it.

I refused to confront her or pick a fight knowing that would give her the opportunity to end up in bed under the constant attendance of her son. Instead I just ignored her. She failed this time to get me riled. I was in a no win situation trying to practice the survival skills of knowing when to let go of things you cannot control.

By the way, I got my ring back years later and the money from it came in very handy. *Bashert.*

Another incident was harder to accept, and took much longer to get over. In fact, it took a month before I stopped having heart palpitations every time I thought about it. Here's what happened.

Over time, our once lovely neighborhood had become unsafe. It became dangerous to walk alone in the streets, even during business hours. People were being robbed in broad daylight. I felt worried and protective, but I did not want to instill fear in my children and hamper their independent growth. My son Dovid was seven when he decided that he wanted to go alone on the city bus to his *Yeshiva.* You can imagine my trepidation, but I finally worked out a system where I could grant his wish. My little daughter and I walked him to the corner and waited with him for the bus. I asked the driver each morning to please keep an eye on him and to make sure he got off at the school. My neighbor's husband picked Dovid up on his way home at the end of the day, and brought him home, together with his own son. This worked out fine until the evening that Dovid did not come home on time. I was beside myself. Of course, Gershon wasn't home. I called the police and they said I had to wait twenty four hours to file a missing persons report. I was frantic. There was nothing I could do while I was worrying, except to make fruitless phone calls. Two hours later, I heard a soft knock at the door and there stood Dovid. In my relief, I yelled at him, "Where have you been?" He said very innocently, "When I got home, Grandma was sitting outside and asked me if I wanted an ice cream." "You went with her without asking me, or calling me?" I answered. But as I spoke to him with unusual sharpness in my voice, I realized that none of this was his fault. In his mind, if his grandmother or any other adult member of the family came for him, it would be okay for him to go with them. They were older and familiar to him, so he thought it would be fine. After I kissed and hugged him and removed his coat, I sat down with him and Avigail and explained to them that they were not allowed to go with anyone, not even a family member, without asking my permission first. "Even if someone says to you that your Mother said it was okay, you must still call me and tell me."

They understood. They were not my problem, my husband and his mother were. Gershon finally came home after spending the hour before dinner with Hodel.

"You should have had a day like I did," I said, and explained what had happened. He ran into his mother's apartment and came back with this excuse. "She said it has been a long time since she had little children, and she didn't think of having Dovid call home." "Sure," I said, "but if you are five minutes late getting to her house, she's ready to faint." And then, I let it pass. There was nothing else I could do except hope that through my children's willingness to obey me, nothing like that could happen again.

In fact, the next evening, Hodel was sitting outside again and my son phoned me to say that she had invited him to go out for ice cream again. He asked if he could go with her. I said "yes" because I wanted to reinforce his good behavior in calling me and I knew he also wanted the ice cream.

I never deprived my children of seeing their grandmother, uncle or cousins. Instilling my negative feelings in them would not have been wise; those issues were adult problems and I wanted to protect my children from conflict. Children identify with their parents and the adults in their immediate family. They easily feel blame if adults quarrel in front of them. I did not want them to feel threatened, insecure, or at fault.

More and more, as incident began to pile upon incident, I realized that the children and I were going to have to leave. I began to think of the life that waited for us, away from my husband's sick family.

✡✡✡

I often thought of how things might have been if Hodel had been willing to work with me instead of against me. Together, we could have had a perfect relationship. She had the keys to our house, access to our lives, my help whenever it was needed, constant contact with her son and grandchildren, and yet she remained sour, manipulative and discontent. I finally realized that if you do *mitzvahs* but everything you do is resented, criticized, and not appreciated, you must eventually sever relations. And that is what I did.

I cut myself off from Hodel completely. To my surprise, this did not sit well with her either. She drove Gershon nuts, wailing and carrying on (which I could not help but overhear from my apartment next door). Of course this kept him tethered to her and interfered with his business. He defended Hodel, but I held to my hard-wrought decision. I worked to keep the environment happy for my children, who still had full access to their grandmother, and I tried to have as little to do with Hodel or Gershon as possible. If my children noticed, they never mentioned it. After all, they had grown up without their father's attention or presence. He was never home, except to wolf down his meals, and he never talked to them about their school, activities or friends. They could not miss what they had never had, and that too was a blessing in disguise.

Chapter 9: What To Tell The Children . . . And Other Advice

When you are in the middle of a bad marriage, it is hard to have a good outlook, but you have to remain calm if only for the sake of your children.

You can't really control the reactions children have to these situations. They will make up their own minds. I decided that I would never speak badly to my children about their father. He was still their father, and always would be. They will feel connected to him, but be assured, their feelings for him will never be as strong as they are for you.

Your main purpose until you can extricate yourself from an unhealthy situation is to make sure you keep yourself and your kids healthy and happy and to keep your home attractive and welcoming. Laugh to your children if your husband goes into a temper tantrum. If he starts throwing things around or acting in a threatening way, pick yourself up and leave with your children.

If he is violent, you can get a restraining order to make him leave and not return. The courts are far more aware these days of how to keep women and children safe in domestic violence situations.

Regardless, you must remain calm, if you can. Tell the children that their father is not well and needs help. If you have had him removed from the home, explain that he will come back when he is well. Try not to upset the children any more than is necessary, they are aware more than you realize.

The tool I found most useful to me was the ability to be decisive. In a crisis, I would stop for a moment and ask myself, "Is this situation in my control or beyond my control?" If I found that the situation was in my control, then I would attempt to set limits and decide what I wanted and expected.

When things were clearly beyond my control, I tried to take a positive mental attitude and willingly let go. At other moments, I had to make myself understand again that everything is *bashert* and that life, in the larger sense, is beautiful. I was very happy in general, especially with my two wonderful children.

The entire purpose of describing these difficult incidents to you, a few out of the thousands I experienced day after day, is to give you a perspective and to encourage you to keep your inner self separate and secure. Your children are watching you and learning from you every minute.

One example: I had befriended a very nice divorced woman named Rivki who had a young son, Josh. We met while taking our children for walks in the park. She was very thin and I worried about her. I often invited her and her son for *Shabbos* at our home. One Thursday, during one of our walks, I stopped in a bakery to buy my challahs and cakes for *Shabbos* and I noticed her looking on with tears in her eyes. I realized she couldn't afford to buy anything, so I whispered to the saleslady to increase my challah and cake order. When we got outside, I said to Rivki, "This bag is so heavy, let me see why." With surprise in my voice I said, "Look at this. She gave me far too much. There is lots more here than I ordered, please do me a favor and take some of this and do with it whatever you want. I hope you'll enjoy with your son for *Shabbos*." She took it with some reluctance, but the tears shining in her eyes told me it was welcome.

My children watched every minute of this transaction. Never underestimate what your kids see and hear; do not forget that you are their only role model, especially if their father is not around to help.

Most of the time, when we entered our home, I'd drop a

•

penny in the charity (*tzedakah*) box. Soon, the children would ask for pennies and they would do the same thing. I would provide the pennies and praise them profusely. As they got older, they would begin to hold doors for people or help neighbors carry heavy shopping bags, and they would say, "My Mommy does this, too. We do *mitzvahs.*"

By the same token, if you laugh off the dumb, mean or silly things your husband, ex-husband or problem relatives do, your children will shrug them off also. Do your own thing and take matters as they come, until the time arrives when events are in your control. Your day will come.

The ultimate objective of a mother is to provide for her children's emotional stability, physical well being and healthy outlook. Play each day as it comes, doing your best. When other adults act badly toward them, try to respond constructively and protectively. When the children get older, they will draw their own conclusions and make their own decisions.

Do not ever instill in them a hatred of their father, because they feel he is a part of them and they will think, subconsciously, that these family problems are their fault, which they are not.

In due time, even if you leave your husband, they will seek him out and get to know him for what he really is. They will form their own opinions. As their mother, you are their strength, their lifeline, their love and their security. Do not weaken your own position; they need you to be strong. You cannot let them down by being vindictive or mean.

The portion we receive in life is G-d given and He does not give us more than we can bear.

Chapter Ten: Going, Going, Gone

Since I had no place to run to with my precious children, I realized I had to bide my time and plan my exodus very carefully. After all, it wasn't only my life that was involved, but more importantly, the welfare of my children.

I saved as much money as I could, making sure we had enough clothes to wear and nice meals to eat. Looking back now, I regret that I didn't sell all our winter clothes (I always knew I'd go to Florida), coats, toys, bikes, and furniture. Gershon was so spaced out, he wouldn't have even noticed if pieces of furniture disappeared. He never noticed that our home was spotless, either. He had been raised in clutter and dirt, and that was his natural expectation. He kept his personal surroundings and his car filthy. I eventually realized that this signified his total lack of self-respect and self-esteem.

When I finally made my decision to leave, I enrolled tiny Avigail in a *yeshiva* pre-school, so that she would have some school group experience. I knew I couldn't depend on Gershon for financial support in the future and if I had to go to work, Avigail would be prepared for *yeshiva*. She loved her nursery school.

The idea of being a happy single mother was a wonderful challenge to me (the idea of being a happy anything would have been a challenge). I knew living independently with my children would offer a far healthier life for all of us, even Gershon.

While my daughter was in *yeshiva* pre-school, I started to work for temporary-help agencies to brush up on my skills. I enjoyed going into different offices. I worked about four hours a day, dropping Avigail off at pre-school, working and returning in time to pick her up. Dovid went to school earlier and came home later, so his routine was never disturbed and, needless to say, I enjoyed having a paycheck at the end of the week.

That last year, after *Pesach*, I started to pack all the things we would need. I told Dovid and Avigail what a wonderful vacation we were going to have. They thought we were going for just a short period of time, but I cherished the joy of planning a new life in a place where there is beauty and sunshine all year long. I also continued to work part-time.

I still remember how busy the children and I were socially that year. We were kept very busy entertaining our friends and accepting numerous invitations, none of which included Gershon. Our close friends all knew that he wasn't really a participant in our lives any longer.

I kept waiting for the children to ask me, "Where is Daddy?" "Why doesn't Daddy come with us?" "Why is Daddy at Grandma's house all the time?" But, thank G-d, they didn't ask. I suppose they thought this was just a normal way of living, although they always saw their friends' fathers at home when they went to play or visit.

My children (this is the proud Mom talking again) were religious, well mannered, well dressed, and a joy to have around. I taught them to have good *midos* and to follow the *Torah* way of life. Socially, they were attentive and polite, so it was easy to take them to restaurants or into my friends' homes. As they matured, I also introduced them to the theater, movies, music and travel.

By *Shavuos*, I finished packing. I still remember how I arranged for three one way train tickets, for us to travel in a comfortable private compartment, from New York City to Miami. I couldn't wait for the day of departure; it was all I could do to hold out until the end of the children's school term.

I must have been a great actress, according to the

neighborhood feedback I got. The last *Shabbos* we were home, we took a family walk, all of us together. We met some members of our synagogue as we strolled. After I left, one of the men we had met told a friend of mine that he had never seen such a happy attractive family in his entire life.

✧✧✧

Did I have doubts about leaving? Of course not. I knew Gershon was mentally ill. I knew his mother was even more so. I knew I had to extricate my children from this environment quickly, while they were still little, to preserve them from harm. I also knew I had to leave for the sake of my own sanity.

Many of my thoughts concerned my own responsibilities, my role as a Jewish woman and mother. I studied and prayed; my resolve and my sense of duty grew with each instance of abuse. I became convinced that the strength of the People of Israel lies within the women. If a mother is happy, no matter where she lives, her children are happy. A mother who lives in the most palatial surroundings but who is depressed all the time cannot raise joyful children, and the atmosphere she creates is depressing.

This also means that material things do not necessarily provide emotional comfort, love or support. For a home to have a healthy environment, even if money is tight, even if there is only one parent, the necessities needed are love, laughter and friends. Children depend on these ingredients to grow into healthy, happy, successful adults without hang-ups.

I saw my role as a mother as psychologically holding my little family together. Responsible men, unlike Gershon, that are good fathers, are role models too. They offer strength, family support, stability, and in that way, they express great love for their families. Of course, fathers can provide deep emotional support but mothers more often express it. In our home, I was the only parent offering or expressing any emotions at all. Gershon could spend ceaseless hours without uttering a word.

Mothers, I believe, were created to protect their children, to be the backbone of civilization. I came to feel that I was providing and could continue to provide this support to my children. And if I had to provide financial support as well, so be it. I could do that too. This would take strength, but not as much as it took to remain where I was.

A single mother can be a successful mother and father role-model. G-d provides us with the coping skills we need. I'm not saying that being a dual role-model is desirable, or the norm, or that it is without stress, but it can be done.

If you are considering leaving an abusive situation, think positively about your own capabilities and your opportunities to regain control of your life. Take things as they come, do not anticipate; G-d will help you if you help yourself.

After a separation, and a divorce, your children's happiness and well-being will continue to take precedence. They will need you and they will keep you busy, coming before your work, your social life, your rest. Trust me, the day will come all too quickly when you will have all the time in the world for solitude and sleep, for thinking about yourself and your needs. This is their time. Be assured, as they grow older, your children will see for themselves all that you have done. My children never had any trouble figuring out who was their true loving parent.

When G-d Himself announced that Sarah, our mother, was to become pregnant and have a son, He made it clear that she would have a decisive influence on the upbringing of her child. By stressing the lead role of the first Jewish mother, a role she was to play alongside her husband, *Torah* makes us conscious of the enormous responsibility which rests upon the Jewish wife and mother. Our sages describe Sarah as a model wife, describing her with King Solomon's words: "*A virtuous woman is a crown to her husband*." He finds his crown in her, not vice versa. Abraham is told (Genesis 21:2), whatever Sarah tells you, heed her. In other words, if a husband listens to his wife's intuition and knowledge, and respects her, and fulfill his duty to her, she will be all to him, his *ezer.* But if he undermines her or weakens her position in the household or harms her, she becomes his *knegdo*, offering the misery Shakespeare describes: "*A woman's wrath is worse than hell.*"

Gershon, who studied a great deal, surely knew this. But I wonder if anything he studied sank in. He prioritized only one commandment, "*Honor your father and your mother.*"Our tradition teaches that honoring one's parents does not mean neglecting one's wife and children. Honoring his mother did not cancel Gershon's wedding vow to forsake all others and cleave only to his wife, and to put his home partnership first. He couldn't do it (because, I believe, he was firmly in the grip of an Oedipus Complex situation and related psychological disorders).

When I first began trying to decide if I should end this unhealthy marriage, I discussed my situation with a Rabbi I respected. (Seeking such professional help, from a Rabbi or professional therapist is a sound first step. Do not turn to your friends to discuss your marriage. You'll ruin the friendship, risk having your confidence betrayed, receive improper emotional and inexpert advice, and destroy your family's privacy. Go to a pro). The Rabbi I spoke to had expertise in situations like mine. He even got angry with me at one point and accused me of doing things for my mother-in-law that I thought were *mitzvahs* but were not, and were truly destructive. He said I hadn't know where a *mitzvah* began and ended, and that I should never have given anyone the key to my house, particularly my mother-in-law, and that I should never have allowed her to move in next door. He explained that honoring parents does not give them the right to control or interfere in their children's lives. They have no right to mix in or become a burden, he said.

The Rabbi and I discussed Hodel's alternatives. I explained that Gershon refused to move away from his mother, due to his attachment to her. I had once suggested a senior citizen's home for her, so she could be busy and occupied all day. But my husband felt Hodel would feel this was just a place to go to wait to die. I told the Rabbi I had argued that sitting alone by a window all day, waiting for her son to pop in and out, was more like waiting for the end. We talked and talked. Ultimately, I told the Rabbi at the end of our session that I thought my mind was made up and that I was going to leave with my children. He gave me his blessing.

When I left with the children, I understood from the grapevine that Hodel was being blamed for the breakup of my marriage. I assumed people had realized that before she moved next to us, we were a happy family, in our home, and in our apartment building. But as soon as she came on the scene, arguments were generated and she was busy turning people against each other. The damage to her reputation came when she could find no way to justify my departure to her friends.

Thus Gershon paid more than one price for being a blindly devoted son: he lost community standing, but more, he lost the precious opportunity to be a devoted father, the head of a happy family. He gave it all to his mother, and it was never enough for her.

We are taught that a man who does not fulfill his responsibilities is a *talmid teepash*, a *chosid shoteh*, and is punished. I realized as I pondered our departure that my husband's punishment for his failure to obey the *Torah* and sustain his family was going to be the loss of his wife and children.

I wasn't sure he would notice that we were gone.

Chapter Eleven: Free At Last

The blessed, long awaited day finally arrived. The children and I were in high spirits and couldn't wait to get on our way. We were looking forward to visiting places like Disney World and Monkey Jungle; swimming every day all day, and shopping. We shared ideas as we used our feet to push our suitcases into the hall.

We stood, waiting for Gershon to leave his mother's apartment and put our bags into the trunk of his car. He emerged from her doorway with a sarcastic smile and told me that Hodel wanted him to take her that same day to the country. He asked if we could delay our departure.

"No," I said clearly, "We have reservations and tickets. We cannot cancel them. We have to leave now."

He delayed us while he told his mother, and finally he loaded the car and took us to the train station. As we prepared for departure, it turned out that he had forgotten his wallet and could give me no cash for the trip. Fortunately I had my own, but he didn't realize that, and I knew that any extra amount would help us.

"I need you to send money every week," I told him.

"Why do you need money?" he asked.

"For food for your children, for expenses," I explained, so exasperated and fed up that I started to laugh. Because I was laughing, the children started to laugh. We boarded the train still laughing, but without the children kissing him or him reaching out to kiss them. When the train pulled away, they didn't even turn to wave good-bye.

✡✡✡

We settled easily into our compartment. The children pressed a bell only to discover that a nice porter came at the sound of its ring and offered to help us. I had brought a delicious barbecue chicken with all the side dishes, so we had a wonderful picnic. The children giggled when they saw our tiny private bathroom and they were delighted with the double-decker beds the porter would open for us that evening.

We went into the lounge and saw a movie. The hostess there gave the children coloring books and crayons. There was even a fashion show. Then we sat and looked out of the picture windows. The children were fascinated with the farms and the cows and other animals they saw as we traveled on our way.

When we returned to our compartment, the children took turns ringing the bell to call the porter to set up our beds. They laughed as if they had seen a magic show when the couch was turned into a bed.

After saying our prayers and sharing lots of hugs and kisses, my two angels fell asleep. I stayed awake, by the window, watching the towns we were passing. I found myself humming and smiling. I finally dozed off, for the first peaceful rest I had enjoyed in a long time.

The porter's cry, "MIAMI, TEN MINUTES," awakened us. We got out of bed quickly and took our turns to wash up and dress in the cute but tiny bathroom. We said our prayers and shared the breakfast I had packed. I rang the porter for coffee, and by the time we had gathered up our belongings, we were pulling into the train station.

We were all drunk with excitement. With great good-byes to our kind porter and newly found friend, and good wishes for all, we piled into the taxi. I had booked us a room in a fine, kosher beachfront hotel for a week of fun. I figured a week would be a nice margin before I began to look for something we could rent and call home for a year. We had a wonderful week of swimming, suntanning, eating and socializing.

Apartment hunting didn't take long. I took a one-year lease on a small but pretty motel-hotel studio in a great location. I particularly liked the wonderful landlords. We moved in, unpacked and continued our vacation, having a great time and making friends.

As the summer ended, I found a wonderful *yeshiva* for the children. As soon as they started school, I got a part time job. Since the High Holidays came early that year, I decided against a full time position. I didn't want to accept a job and then immediately pile up a lot of absences. But after *Simhas Torah*, G-d led me to a perfect job in a fundraising office. The salary would support us comfortably, even though I would be working under considerable stress and pressure. I kept that job for twelve years. One of the best benefits about it was that my boss accepted my request to let me leave work at four p.m. if I didn't take a lunch hour.

From the beginning, when Avigail was only six, I was home when she got out of school. My son, who took extra Judaic studies classes, came home a couple of hours later.

We led a wonderful, even glamorous life. My son went fishing with a kind older man who had befriended us. My daughter and I went shopping for clothes or food. We all went swimming and, after a while, I bought them bikes so we could go biking together as well.

Dovid and Avigail did great in school. They would do their homework after dinner each night and were eager to go back to school the next day. I looked forward to going to the office, and after just a couple of months, we had a happy routine.

It had long since become clear to the children that we were not going home, but they never asked about their father. In fact, they did not mention him once after we arrived in Miami. I finally suggested that they talk to him on the phone. I told them to give him our address and telephone number so he would know where to send the weekly check he had promised. He said "okay," when Dovid gave him the address. That was the sickest "okay" in the history of the language. His idea of okay could be a month, a year or never. Needless to say, it often took several phone calls to remind him. I finally insisted on a monthly check, figuring it would be easier to remember twelve times a year rather than fifty two times.

✡✡✡

Gershon's behavior didn't vary as our status changed; from wife and children on vacation to ex-wife and children living in Florida. He didn't care before our divorce, which I obtained three years after we moved to Florida, and he didn't care afterwards.

According to prevailing law in most states, a wife is entitled to half of her husband's business or estate. She is also often given alimony, child support, insurance and school tuition.

I suppose I could have demanded the same arrangement that Lana got from Shlomo, who wasn't president of the company, and not divorced. My ex-sister-in-law's rent was paid, she had spending money, her children's tuition was covered and she dressed beautifully. She never worked a day. Meanwhile, Shlomo maintained two apartments (Lana's and Hodel's), sent his children to overnight camp, drove a Lincoln car, spent all the *yom tovim* at fine hotels, took a great summer vacation every year and, sent his mother to the country annually. Gershon was also living well, driving a Cadillac, taking fancy holidays and spending the summer with his mother in the mountains. I also could have demanded my engagement ring and the money that had been stolen from my bank account.

After three years, we finally reached the stage where my

attorney and I could meet with Gershon and his lawyer and finalize our settlement. When the meeting was set, I made it clear that I had to leave by three thirty p.m. to pick up Avigail.

I tried to be calm. I knew two important things: first, Gershon was so immature and irresponsible that he could not be depended upon, and second, that G-d would take care of me and would be sure I had what I needed. If I was meant to have it, *Hashem* would guarantee it. And if I wasn't, it was *bashert*.

I asked my lawyer to buffer me from Gershon. I didn't want to ever see him again. I couldn't stand being in the same room with him as he hung his head and pleaded poverty, totally unconcerned with his children though he was still supporting every Rabbi who sought charity from him. The meeting dragged on and on.

I finally left, just as Gershon was claiming that he couldn't afford more than twenty five dollars per child per week, and that he couldn't pay their full *yeshiva* tuition.

To make a long story short, my exhausted attorney called me a few weeks later and said he had never dealt with anyone as immature and obnoxious as my ex-husband. He said he was closing the case. I felt a great burden lift from my chest. Gershon would remain in my life because he was the father of my children, but my relationship with him was formally severed.

After the divorce, my children and I found that our lives remained content and everything went on as if nothing major had happened.

Chapter Twelve: A Few Thoughts On Divorce

Before I share with you the challenging years I spent raising my children, I want you to know that the specific idea for this book didn't come to me until years after my divorce. I first thought of it during the exhilarating night after my son's wedding, when my joy and excitement kept me awake far into the night. Even before I left New York, even as I held the return train tickets to Florida, I knew G-d would not have tested me without a reason.

My miserable marriage had to have a purpose. I knew G-d had a reason for the years he had me spend with a sick man, and to try to conceal his illness from our children. Everything is meant to be. Maybe the children, themselves, were the reason I had to suffer through eight years with this dreadful man. The children would be reason enough. From a negative always comes a positive, and perhaps it was my destiny to pay eight years of unhappiness in order to obtain many years of untold joy from these two wonderful people, their spouses and children.

Then again, maybe this book is also part of the reason. Perhaps *Hashem*, who gives us all a portion, but never gives us more than we can bear, gave me this lot in my life to make me stronger, to continue to build my complete faith and trust in Him so that I could reach out to other women. This book is for all abused, miserably married Orthodox women who find themselves in loveless, dead-end marriages that steal from them the familial joy our beautiful religion promises. Most Orthodox marriages are happy, because they are based on *Torah*. But in these modern times, even the poison of abuse has seeped into our homes, and those women being harmed by this poison are the women I hope to help.

I want to share my story with women who are too frightened to pick up with their children and leave their emotional, physical and mentally unhealthy environment. I know that this book can fulfill the greatest *mitzvah Hashem* ever gave me the strength to do: the *mitzvah* of offering these women the strength to change their lives.

Divorce is never something to advocate, but if divorce is needed, perhaps I can help them approach it with a positive attitude and *bitochon* that they will survive to lead a better life. I want these women to know that there can be happiness after a divorce.

If you remain with an abusive husband out of fear or because you accept sole responsibility for his unacceptable behavior because of his brain-washing you are buying into his sickness. Blaming you for his sickness (with such statements as, "I wouldn't have hit you if you didn't make me") is absolutely against the teachings of our holy *Torah*. If you are being abused you must muster every ounce of courage, believe in the sacredness of your own body and thoughts, and confide in a Rabbi or professional therapist.

Your path to departure may be slow, particularly if the abuse you are suffering is mental and emotional, but if you are physically abused, for G-d's sake, leave immediately, especially if your children witness such behavior. Go to the nearest emergency room, or women's shelter (please G-d, a shelter for Orthodox women, if there is one near you). I assure you, you cannot reason with an out-of-control abusive husband. If you find yourself in this situation, get our of your home immediately.

This is no time to worry about your reputation or about your children's *shidduchim* or about your grandmother's silver candlesticks; this is a time to save your life so grab your children and leave. Yes, it will be hard on the children, but not nearly as hard as remaining where there is physical abuse and under the care of a sad and terrified mother.

Therapists know the reasons women remain trapped in abusive marriages. Don't fall prey to these excuses. They are genuine worries, but they can be overcome. Why do women remain in dead-end marriages? Because:

1. They have no means of financial support.
2. Orthodox women are sometimes not brought up to be self-supporting. Often they are married at a very young age with no formal education and no way to make a living.
3. Some women see divorce as a failure, a stigma.
4. They fear the uncertain future, and they fear not being accepted because they are divorced.
5. They have no place to go, no home, food or security.
6. They fear evil gossip and lies; they feel ashamed.
7. They fear seeking outside help (though this may be their first productive step). They fear openly admitting their problems. Many women ignore and deny their situation with the hope that the problems will just go away. They continue in a miserable marriage as matters worsen.
8. They fear the difficulty of getting a *get* and a fair settlement.
9. They fear traumatic custody battles.
10. They fear that they will ruin their children's chances of good *shidduchim*. If you remain in a horrible, abnormal situation, your children will not only be hampered in meeting good potential mates, they will be emotionally scarred with all the hang-ups that abuse causes, emotional illnesses that will follow them into adulthood and marriage.

These are real fears. You can't dismiss them, but you can survive them.

The stories one hears of difficulties in receiving a *get* would make the brave tremble. A Jewish woman cannot remarry without a *get*, a religious divorce decree, even though she's legally divorced. I was in no real rush for a *get* because dating and remarriage were never in my plans. So when my Rabbi called me and said that Gershon had given him my *get*, he urged me to come pick it up. I told the Rabbi I wished he had informed me before the proceedings because I wanted Gershon, who also needed a *get* to remarry, to pay me for granting it. He had gotten away with depriving me and his children in our divorce settlement and the *get* would have given me a bargaining tool. The Rabbi said he didn't want to get involved in any sticky situation. At his response, my instinct told me to just pick up my *get* and be done with it, so I did. It was a relief to have one more step completed, like getting rid of a chronic illness. The Rabbi mentioned nothing about my request and seemed anxious for me to leave. I decided that G-d had never let me down and that this had happened for a reason.

The following day, a friend in New York called me. She knew the *sofer,* the scribe, who had prepared the *get*. She was told that the *sofer* "never witnessed such an emotional scene in his life." I was told that Gershon was hysterical, that he couldn't stop crying and kept repeating that he loved his wife and children but was obsessed with being abnormally in love with his mother and couldn't help it. Apparently the Rabbi thought Gershon was beyond any psychiatric intervention and supplied the *get*. But every *get* has it's own story. If you need to leave, this is just another barricade you will have to surmount with faith.

No one pretends that this is ever easy. Re-establishing yourself financially is extremely difficult. You face the real threat of lies, gossip and *loshen hora* from an ex-husband and his family and friends. Society frowns on divorce, and Orthodox Jewish society in particular views it as a failure overloaded with guilt and shame. The understanding that divorce is a *shanda* comes from our

European great-grandparents, who lived in simpler, not easier, but simpler times. That this kind of shame would be brought upon a family was unheard of. They kept their problems in the closet so it would not affect a future *shidduch.*

Just keep your eye on a core truth: if you remain in a consistently abusive situation, you are not only endangering your own life, mind, body and soul, but those of your children. If a woman finds herself trapped in a loveless marriage, the *Torah* itself advocates divorce. Stories that mirror my loveless, and sexless marriage are unfortunately becoming more prevalent today. Our Rabbis know that a marriage cannot be held together without physical closeness, attraction and bonding, the joining of two individuals into one happy, whole unit.

If you are in this situation, give much thought over time, and you may come to decide that you need a divorce. And if you truly need one, if talking and trying and counseling and hoping all fail, then you must get one. Divorce can be the medicine that cures a destructive disease.

Try not to dwell on the negativity. You **WILL** get through these issues one at a time, day by day. Try to keep your mind and heart on the positive outcome and renew your faith in *Hashem.* Believe in your own second chance, in a new beginning in life. Believe always that you and your children will survive this test with G-d's help and guidance. Believe in your own self-worth. Divorce is frightening, but not as frightening as living through a marriage that will incapacitate you, rob you of your health and ability to raise your children, or put your lives in danger.

Step one is to come to the realization, after all possible avenues of reconciliation have been explored, that the marriage is over and there is no hope of salvaging it. Step two, plan for your freedom. Step three, see a Rabbi or therapist. And then, see a lawyer.

I had left New York when our separation and pending

divorce became public knowledge. The children and I left as if we were going on vacation, only our continued absence made our family's situation clear. I advocate doing this if you can, if only to shield yourself from ugly gossip.

However, an abusive home rarely remains a secret forever. It is an unhealthy environment which poisons the people within it. Your children are victims and will manifest signs of abuse through their behavior. These problems will reveal themselves in school, in the eyes of observant teachers and guidance counselors. Your friends, and their friends, will notice signs of abuse and neglect. Then the thing you most wanted to hide will become the subject on everyone's mind. If leaving is going to be necessary, leave while you are still well, while your children are still whole and healthy.

Dovid was eight and Avigail was six when we left, just in time. When we settled into our little studio in Florida that first year, I did not know what was in my future, I only knew that I finally had a future again, and that I was going to reach out for it.

Chapter Thirteen: Childhood in Florida

We stayed in our lovely little motel studio for a year. We became very close to the husband and wife team who owned the motel; we loved each other like family. They had just sold their New York business and moved to Florida. The motel was a new venture for them, and I wanted to help. I offered to handle their correspondence and reservations. My son learned how to manage the switchboard, so they could take a dinner break when he got home from school, and even little Avigail stuffed envelopes and licked the flaps. When they visited New York, we held down the fort. Once, they even bought Dovid a new fishing rod. They traveled from New York with a fishing rod, such love. To this day, there isn't anything we wouldn't do for each other.

Unfortunately, I soon began to realize that the children and I needed a more permanent environment. We made many friends among the motel's guests, but they were all transient. As soon as we got close, they went back to their hometowns, leaving us with lots of letter writing and memories. My children did not need to undergo any more separations; it just wasn't wholesome for them. I began to look for an apartment.

Just before we moved from the studio, a girlfriend of mine in New York called and warned me that Gershon was planning a surprise visit. Instead of calling to find out if his timing would disrupt their school schedule, he intended to just appear. I was grateful for my friend's call because it enabled me to prepare Avigail and Dovid, instead of having them startled and upset.

I told them I thought their father was going to surprise us

with a visit. I explained that since our motel was booked up, and our studio was too tiny for him to stay with us, he would sleep at the hotel and visit with us. This seemed to satisfy them. They ate with him at the hotel, toured with him around town and seemed glad to see him.

We had one bad day during the visit when Dovid suggested that we rent a boat. I suggested hiring someone to sail it, since Gershon had never done anything like that before, but he refused to relinquish the chance to be a big-shot. My nightmares have engraved that boat ride permanently into my memory. Gershon sailed the boat like a fast car, not knowing anything about the rules of the water. The boat had no life rafts and Gershon handled the steering wheel so roughly that it fell off. We screamed for help to a passing boat, which radioed the rental office. They sent out a second boat, which Avigail and I boarded. That boat then towed the one we rented, with Dovid and Gershon aboard. I took a picture because no one would have believed the story otherwise. Luckily, my children remember the outing as a fun afternoon and no permanent fear was instilled in them. But I couldn't wait for Gershon to leave so we could resume our new peaceful lives.

Of course, when he left, he forgot to leave a check for the food. He continued to visit twice a year, always disrupting our lives and schedules. After that first visit, he always brought his mother with him and told my children not to tell me she was here. They never lied, and certainly would not at his behest, but I understood that he came primarily because Hodel wanted a Florida vacation. The children believed he came for them, and I let them think so, because it made them feel good. As a single parent, I had to prepare myself to handle my children after he left them on a high, satiated with goodies, their routine totally destroyed. I had to readjust my actions based on their reactions to these disruptive occasions.

At the end of one summertime visit, Gershon was telling

the children good-bye while his mother waited in the car. My daughter was upset and asked her father to stay one more day, but his mother kept urging him to hurry up or they would miss their plane. When they pulled away, Avigail came to me with a tear-stained face. I quickly kissed her and held her close. I said, "Come on, sweetheart. Let's go shopping. Wash your pretty face, and while we shop we can sit down and have a soda and talk about your fun visit with your father." In about an hour, she was her old self again and, on her own, she changed our conversation to other subjects. Dovid came home to join us and called up a friend to play basketball. He didn't seem affected at all. But the conclusion of each visit was different; I had to learn to play it all by ear.

✡✡✡

When we left the studio, I reluctantly moved us to an apartment in a residential area, farther from our real needs. I couldn't find anything closer, since every landlord I met refused to take children. I signed a year lease and vowed to keep looking. We made the best of it and continued our way of life, enjoying sports, plays, movies, friends, travel, parties and holiday gatherings. But all the while, I kept looking for an apartment closer to our synagogue, their school, my office, and our friends.

By the end of our second year, I found it: a cute little apartment in just the right location. With much thanks to *Hashem*, the children and I moved in. Everything was fun and games. My two little blessings were happy and rarely asked about their father at all.

With only my income to rely upon, we were really below the poverty level, but we never felt poor. Our value system and our ability to have fun kept us feeling on top of the world.

Birthday parties are a prime example of how we enjoyed ourselves. In spite of my super-economical ways and conservative spending, I never regretted giving delightful surprise birthday parties for my son and daughter. I have beautiful pictures (which my grandchildren love to look at) and memories of their happy faces. Even when I didn't have any money for even a small party, I'd borrow a bit and pay it back quickly. Every year we did something different, something happy, something together to make their birthdays special.

As we created a new life for ourselves, with birthdays and other happy events, the children mentioned Gershon less frequently, and only in the wake of his bi-annual visits. Support checks came from him sporadically. Although I no longer spoke to him, the children did phone him now and then. Each time, I asked them to nudge him about sending the money. Still, with frugal care, I managed to keep a nice apartment, dress myself and the children beautifully, take vacations, entertain, give appropriate *bar* and *bas mitzvah* and wedding presents, and maintain a nice lifestyle. Because I paid for everything promptly, I had excellent credit. I joined the credit union and was able to save some money in a private bank account. When the twenty five dollars per week for each child failed to arrive, I borrowed and paid it back promptly. I tried hard never to criticize Gershon to the children.

One Sunday, when Dovid was about eleven years old, I noticed that he was unusually quiet. I started to talk to him and suddenly his tears began to flow. I believe that the American culture is the only one that professes that it is weak for men to cry, thus creating a society of macho-types who cannot release their emotions. European culture encourages men (and women) to cry and to kiss each other, to hug, to express their feelings. Crying releases suppressed emotions and feelings of stress and pressure.

As I held Dovid, I said intuitively, without even asking about school or his friends, "Boobah, do you miss Daddy?" He nodded his head. I told him, "Cry first and then we'll talk." I held him closely and whispered into his ear, "Keep crying if you want to. I love you. And if you want to call Daddy on the phone, you can do that any time."

Dovid did call his father. I didn't hear what was said, but that was the first and last episode of that kind that we experienced together.

That same day, when Avigail came home from the friend's home she was visiting, I told both children, "You know you have a lot of stress in school with lots of homework, and you have had many changes in your life. If you want to release the stress, you can either kick a ball, talk about it with me, or, if you feel like crying, you can cry, with me or in the bathroom with the door closed. Remember that your father is only a phone call away. You can call him, or write him. He is still your father." They listened, but they didn't have much to say.

I found it unusual that my children never asked for Gershon, except for Dovid this one time. The only reason I could find was that he had never been close to them in the first place, so they had no deep emotional ties to him.

✡✡✡

I always told Dovid and Avigail to bring their friends to our home. During the week, our apartment was filled with the sounds of their laughter.

Our apartment had a cute living room, a pretty dining room and a studio-type bedroom that was meant for fun. It was piled high with weights, an exercise bench, tennis racquets, and fishing rods, with baseball bats propped behind the door. Both children had beautiful furniture, including a desk, a hutch and a dresser. My son's bed had six drawers on the bottom, to give him plenty of room for his baseball card and stamp collections. I had an extra bookcase built for Avigail when she entered high school to hold all her books; she loved to read and could never give up a favorite volume after she finished it. Avigail also had a beautiful desk, hutch and lingerie chest.

The purchase of our furniture included the advice of a decorator who taught me to hang plenty of shelves on the walls and use all the extra corners and behind-the-door spaces. We bought our furniture and the apartment was done in earth tones with a couch, club chairs, an etagere filled with mementos, an artificial tree, a stereo, a television and an extension table so more guests could join us for meals. Our home seemed to stretch for company, proving only that if you want friends to join you, you can make it happen. If you want to make room, you can. I bought stack tables for the children to nosh on, and they came to respect our sweet small home. No one ever jumped on the furniture or put their feet on the coffee table; they just understood the atmosphere I tried to create.

Even though some of my children's friends lived in palatial houses, they seemed to like to congregate in our apartment. Why? Because we made them welcome and showed them love and affection. We just asked that food be eaten only at the table and that crumbs be vacuumed up quickly, so that we could stay bugless (a tough task in the tropics). The children told me that at other fancier homes, they weren't allowed to go into the kitchen because it might upset the maid if they left a cup by the sink or splashed a little water. They had to take their shoes off. They felt very constrained amid the luxury. This confirmed my conviction that children only want love, comfort and care, as opposed to material goods offered without sustaining affection. True emotional support and the love of a fun-loving, serene parent is what counts.

My son and daughter would take turns inviting friends for *Shabbos*. One week, Dovid would have one or two boys stay with us, and the next week, Avigail's girlfriends would come. When their friends visited from out of town, they always stayed with us.

My first piece of new furniture was a couch that opened up to be a bed where three or four little girls could spend the night.

I tried to make sure that our *Shabbos* table was abundant, with plenty of food children like. Once my son had a friend visiting from Texas who asked with wonder, "Does you mother always cook this much?" I was forced to admit that the answer was yes.

Our *Shabbosim* were a joy. I would get up very early, four thirty a.m. on Fridays, put in a load of laundry, start cooking for *Shabbos*, and set the table. By seven thirty, I would wake up the children, and at eight a.m. we left, with the cooking done for ourselves and our company, and our home ready for *Shabbos*. I could leave the office at four p.m. knowing that everything was prepared. We enjoyed our *Shabbosim* and *yom tovim* with friends, who often invited us to their homes to share celebrations.

One night I received a call from a woman who literally begged me to invite her nine-year-old son for *Shabbos*. She said he loved my son and wanted to spend a *Shabbos* in our home. I assured her that he was always welcome. He was a pleasure to have around, and he joined us often.

Today that nine-year-old is an important real estate tycoon. He always reminds me of the *Shabbosim* he spent in my home. When he and my son's other grown-up friends come to call, they gravitate to the back bedroom, which was set up like a studio for them to enjoy. With a pensive, emotional expression on their faces, they uniformly look around and whisper, "What memories!!" My daughter's friends say they can't believe they are bringing their children to play in the same room they loved as children. Their joy brings joy to me, and helps me keep wonderful memories and past experiences alive. My photo gallery is filled with their happy faces.

While my children were growing up, they made wonderful friends and grew in *midos* and *derech eretz*. Their sterling personalities began to emerge and I was very proud of their fine characters (of course, as a mother, my opinion is very objective!).

Dovid and Avigail's intense *yeshiva* education began early in the mornings and ended late, with about three hours a night of homework. The *yeshiva* program prepares observant children for life and builds their self-esteem and self-respect. They don't have time to hang around street corners and get in trouble. They seem to grow up healthy and normal despite the pressures.

Avigail usually got out of school fifteen minutes before the end of my work day, so the school bus dropped her at my office. My friends came to love her bubbly personality. We went shopping after I finished work, and by the time Dovid came home from *yeshiva*, we had supper on the table. We even enjoyed the time after supper, when they did homework and I busied myself cleaning the apartment. I was, and still am, a night person, so I did all the cleaning in the evening. That left our days open for working, learning and having fun. Our days and nights were filled with joy.

As you can tell from the list of sports equipment that piled up in my small room, I encouraged their extra-curricular activities as they developed. The children didn't really have much time for energy-releasing sports or fulfilling artistic pursuits during the school year, especially since their school met even for a half-day on Sunday, so we took advantage of the summer months as well as rare after-school hours.

I think a good extra-curricular program helped Dovid and Avigail manage their scholastic challenges. I encouraged various lessons and extra-curricular activities because I believe that every child has a G-d given talent, in sports, arts, volunteer work, or some other endeavor, that a parent should seek, recognize and nurture.

For instance, my son's interest in playing the guitar stemmed from a toy guitar I bought him when he was only two. After we moved to Florida, he continued to express an interest in the guitar. I hired the best guitar instructor in the community to teach him, at ten dollars an hour, which was a lot of money for me at the time. The teacher confirmed my sense that Dovid had tremendous musical talent, so the investment in his future was worthwhile. After his second lesson, the teacher evaluated him so highly that he took Dovid under his wing. He became so involved with Dovid that he never looked at the clock during a lesson. After three months, he told me to get Dovid an electric guitar and an amplifier. By age twelve, my son, G-d bless him, was already playing in orchestras, accompanying singers and making a few dollars for himself. (Now that he's married and the father of three, the extra money from a few guitar-playing assignments each month still comes in very handy).   When Dovid graduated from high school, the Rabbi called him to receive his diploma by introducing him as the smiling guitarist.

Avigail tried the guitar and didn't care for it. Her artistic talent was more visual; she had a talent for painting. To encourage her, I bought her paints, brushes and fine paper, and she was in her glory. Avigail's other great love is children. She became the best loved and most in-demand baby-sitter in our area. Parents who were coming to the kosher hotels in Miami Beach from all over the country would call to book her in advance. This gift of caring for children led Avigail to an adult career in special education, so I always felt that her baby-sitting hours were well spent.

Until Dovid and Avigail reached *bar* and *bas mitzvah* age, they went to summer day camp so that their minds were occupied constructively during the vacation months. After age thirteen, Avigail baby-sat in the summers. Dovid, after morning *yeshiva* classes, worked in a coffee shop in a local hotel, worked as a pool boy, and ran a booth in one of the down-town hotels where, Coney Island style, he would blow up balloons for children who would pop them to win prizes.   He was taught how to lay tile floors, which came in handy later on in his married life.

Working gives children a fantastic sense of self-esteem and

productivity. It also teaches them how to manage their time and their money, a big plus for the future.

We always ended the summers by taking a three week vacation together so that the children returned refreshed and ready for the school year.

Chapter 14: Jewish Life in Florida

The advent of the first of the Jewish holidays since we moved to Florida brought my own special prayer to G-d to help me survive the holiday season. With determination and a continued smile on my face I worked hard to cover up the fact that my children were going to be fatherless for the holiday season ahead. Judaism commands a father to share the laws of each holiday with his son, if he has one. The one time a visit would have been appropriate, Gershon spent his holidays at a mountain hotel with his mother.

I kept us busy with the excitement of the holidays by shopping for new clothes, giving the house a special cleaning, choosing which friends we would have for dinner and whose invitations we would accept. All in all, I tried to keep the spirit in our home high and happy.

The High Holidays

The only telephone call that came from Gershon before the holidays, from the mountains where he was with Hodel, was enough to bring out the hatred I had within me for this so-called father-Rabbi, who didn't want to share the most holy season of the year with his children.

As soon as the quick phone call was over, the children came running to help with the setting of our *Rosh Hashanah* table which was replete with all the special kinds of foods, a lovely starched special tablecloth, and shiny dishes. G-d's spirit imbued the atmosphere in our home.

My son dressed in one of his many new suits and, looking

like a king, went to *shul* for the evening prayers and walked home
with our guests. My beautiful daughter and I also dressed for the
holidays and were busy with the final touches of preparing the
salads, desserts, and more.

Rosh Hashanah and *Yom Kippur* are the two most
awesome holidays of the Jewish calendar. During these holidays, a
father plays a very important role especially in the relationship
with his son. At the end of the Sabbath before *Rosh Hashanah*
there is a special midnight service called "*Selichos*," when a son
needs a father's presence because of the various customs the *Torah*
demands of the father. I must admit that if I thought my children
were in need of a male role model, I would have considered
adopting a very fine childless couple and would have made them
their foster grandparents. But thank G-d, G-d gave me the strength
to be both father and mother and we all went to *shul* for the
selichos service with our friends. Thank G-d, my children did not
show any signs of missing a father.

On the beautiful day of *Rosh Hashanah*, I was honored to
bless my children myself. We were excited because we were
looking forward to having our guests enjoy our delicious food and
share in the *simcha* of the holiday. When my daughter and I arrived
at *shul* for the morning prayers, we saw Dovid smiling and sitting
with his friends.

The moment I was dreading came too quickly. The most
beautiful custom, the priests' blessing, calls for fathers to put their
prayer shawls around themselves and their sons. I was watching
my son as he looked around at all his friends being wrapped in
their fathers' shawls. He looked up to me and I smilingly motioned
him to come upstairs so that he could stand with me and his sister
while we were all being blessed. Dovid was the only boy in the
whole synagogue without a father present, but I handled it very
nonchalantly. Coming upstairs to be with me seemed to satisfy him
that day.

The second day, some of his friends fathers' were not there, so those boys without fathers took some prayer shawls and wrapped themselves with the shawls to receive the priestly blessing.

Also on the second day of *Rosh Hashanah*, the special custom of "*Tashlich*" is observed. Families gather beside small streams of water one of which happened to be in our backyard. We all got together after the holiday meal, my guests, my children, and me, and we said the necessary prayers and then emptied our pockets of our sins and threw them into the water. We have fond memories of this custom to this day.

After *Rosh Hashanah* was over, I asked my son if he could ask his father to come to Florida for *Yom Kippur*. Gershon said no, and told Dovid that for future holidays, he should stand in a corner while the priestly blessings were in progress. You can come to your own conclusions, especially from the perspective of men who are blessed with sons; is this the way a normal father acts to his son? Then again, I can't help but be convinced that Gershon really was very ill, and thank G-d, there wasn't close contact between father and son. Who knows what kind of garbage he would have fed my son and how my son would have reacted. Everything is meant to be and there is a blessing involved even though it is too hidden for us to recognize at the time. It reveals itself in due time. Be patient. The answer of standing in a corner didn't seem to bother my son.

Yom Kippur

The eve of *Yom Kippur* has another special father and child ceremony, where the father blesses his children. I was able to perform this *mitzvah*, wishing my children long, healthy, happy, religious lives. I must point out again that not once since we lived in Florida and during all the holidays, did my children ask me where their father was. They never knew my inner feelings of sadness for them and hatred for their father, even as we walked to *shul* together for the beautiful *Kol Nidre* service.

Succos

During the festive holiday of *Succos*, my daughter decorated our *succah* built by my friend's husband. I bought my son a *lulov* and the most beautiful *esrog* with its own silver box. My daughter and I watched him walk proudly around the *shul*. All of his friends asked to borrow his *lulov* and *esrog*. I made a donation to the *shul* from my children and we were invited out as guests for the last two days of *Succos*, which was lots of fun. After services, we entered the large and beautifully decorated *shul succah* for a wonderful *Succos kiddush*. All the women had a chance to say their blessings over the *lulov* and *esrog*. My friends used our house to wash for the *motzie* and serve the food, so again my house was the center of all activity and happy memories. All I remember is laughter and jokes and happy faces. My children were ecstatic to be able to be hosts to all our friends.

Simchas Torah

President Kennedy once made a remark that because of his back injury he would never know the thrill of giving his children a piggy back ride and his children would never know what it would be like to have their father give them a piggy back ride. My son and daughter never knew what it was like to have a piggy back ride on their father's back while all their friends were having a wonderful time with their fathers, carrying flags, dancing and singing in celebration of *Simchas Torah*. I solved the problem very easily by asking one of the bigger boys to give Dovid and Avigail a little piggy back ride, since little girls are also involved in this holiday. My children were thrilled with the intricate dancing the teenager did while they took turns on his back. I only saw happy smiling faces and the holiday was a joy to all of us. I made a special donation so my son could walk around the *shul* with a *Torah* during the special *hakofos* ceremony and he walked like a regal king. We were so proud of him. All of his friends surrounded him like a court of escorts and they were all singing and dancing.

Chanukah

For *Chanukah,* we made potato latkes, played dreidel, spent time with our friends, and shared homes for parties for this eight-day holiday. My children lit the candles and every night another friend who was visiting lit the newest candle. I have beautiful pictures and memories of this holiday.

Purim

On *Purim,* Avigail baked delicious *hamentashen* and we had the *seudah* in our house. We went to the synagogue on the eve of *Purim* to hear the *megillah* and we also went on the morning of the holiday. My son and daughter gave out their *shalach monos* gift baskets to our friends while I prepared for the *seudah* which would be in our home later that afternoon. We also received *shalach monos* in return. On the morning of *Purim,* my children's *yeshiva* put on a costume party. My daughter won for the beautiful bride (*Queen Esther*) costume that I had made for her one year. My eyes still fill with tears at the memory of little Avigail in the white frilly bride dress. Again a joyous holiday with wonderful memories for a lifetime.

Pesach

Pesach, the most beautiful holiday in the Jewish calendar, is the hardest for women. My daughter and I stripped our house to make sure there was no leaven in the pockets, or suitcases, or drawers, or in any of the books. My son took care of the traditional search for the *chometz*, the sale of the *chometz* and the burning of the *chometz*.

On the morning of *erev Pesach*, a first born son has to attend a very important service in memory of redeeming the first born. This service is usually shared with a father, but Dovid had friends whose fathers were also missing so it didn't seem to bother them that they were all together, fatherless. The excitement of shopping, cooking, and setting the table occupied us, because the first *seder* was in our house. We were invited out for the second one. My daughter said the four questions and both children had fun stealing the *afikomen* and bargaining for its return.

I remember one year my daughter asked me how her father would hear her say the four questions if he wasn't with us. I said, "He will hear you, sweetheart". This seemed to satisfy her.

Shavuos

On *Shavuos*, Avigail made delicious cheesecake and *blintzes*. My son spent the eve of the holiday with his friends in the synagogue learning until the next morning. We had the evening meal at our house the first night and the second night we were invited out. The weather is very spring like and we all looked attractive in our new festive clothing. Beautiful memories again, remain with us.

All holidays, and all birthday parties, were a tremendous part of our lives in Florida and everything is imprinted in our memories and in our picture albums with loving remembrance. All in all, my children felt lots of love all around them and happiness in every corner of their lives.

Shabbos

Shabbos, our most beautiful gift from *Hashem*, was the one day we longed for all week long. It started with our joyous Friday night meals with friends and then *Shabbos* morning services, followed by a *kiddush* and then lunch at a friend's house. In the afternoon came *Shabbos* learning groups for my children and a *talmudic* discussion with our Rabbi for me and my friends, and then going into my friend's house for coffee and *shelosh seudos.* *Havdalah,* which ends the sabbath, was a letdown. We didn't want *Shabbos* to leave, that's how much we loved it.

We also enjoyed basketball games on Saturday nights at the convention hall, or concerts, or movies. Then on Sunday there was school for half a day and in the afternoon we went to some fun place. By Monday, we were all ready for school and work with a feeling of fulfillment and joy for the past *Shabbos* and, of course, we were looking forward and making plans for the next *Shabbos* and enjoying the week ahead.

✡✡✡

Of all the special times I remember, the most moving event came five years after we moved to Miami: Dovid's *bar mitzvah*, followed two years later by Avigail's memorable *bas mitzvah*. These wonderful events brought me much joy.

Dovid's *Bar Mitzvah*
My daughter, our friends and I were all looking forward to that very special day when my son would be called to the *Torah* for his *bar mitzvah*. According to Jewish law a boy becomes a man in the eyes of the *Torah*, which commands him to fulfill the commandments that were handed down to the People of Israel at Mt. Sinai. It is also a very emotional moment for the parent when you see your son continuing the unbroken chain of our beautiful heritage.

In normal situations, this *simcha* is shared by both parents. For a religious man to have a son attain this goal, it is supposed to be the ultimate of all blessings. But here I was planning a beautiful affair and having to deal with a fool instead of a father.

I hired a very nice Rabbi to teach my son his *haftorah*, and I leased the synagogue's new social hall for a congregational *kiddush*. I also hired an orchestra and photographer for the evening affair. On my end, things were great.

Avigail helped her brother select special invitations. She and I bought matching dresses and I ordered two new suits for Dovid.

Out of the blue, Gershon called and said he would pay for half of the affair and one of my son's new suits. I told him which deposits to send to the various people involved. I was just as glad that he wanted to participate financially, although he never came down to see how Dovid was doing or to hear him practice his *haftorah* or *bar mitzvah* speech.

The blessed day arrived. Gershon didn't offer to pick up Dovid because he was occupied escorting, in fact, holding up, his ailing mother. Poor, sick woman; poor, sick son.

Dovid was happy although he felt nervous like most *bar mitzvah* boys. When the time came, he performed magnificently. Avigail and I were so proud of him. My friends all wished me *mazel tov* as we entered the synagogue's decorated social hall for a delicious *kiddush.*

The only part of the *bar mitzvah* I found hard to take were all the undeserved honors and congratulations that went to Gershon. I thought it was unjust for a neglectful parent to walk into a lovely affair and get such unearned *naches.* I steeled myself and refused to let such thoughts spoil Dovid's special day.

The evening affair was a splendid party. Everyone had a wonderful time dancing, singing, eating, and just enjoying themselves. The orchestra was outstanding and the faces of my guests expressed their happiness. The pictures came out perfect, just the right accompaniment to my memories, which contain every single image, from beginning to end.

Part of the reason I have such nice memories is that I ignored Gershon and Hodel completely. In the event that Gershon hadn't shown up, I was prepared to have one of Dovid's teachers stand in for him.

After the guests had left, Gershon had the audacity to take the orchestra leader aside and argue and bargain for a lower fee, even though he had signed the orchestra's contract. This is totally against Jewish law. We are not allowed to cheat anyone of honest profit after a contract has been signed, although before that, bargaining is legitimate.

I would caution anyone in a similar situation. Don't let one person's sourness spoil your *simcha* or upset you. Gershon tried. The day after the *bar mitzvah*, he had only negative things to say.

Of course, he was repeating the jealous ravings of his depressed, sickly mother. I couldn't wait for both of them to get out of town.

The most important star of the show was Dovid, who performed extraordinarily, considering how nervous he was. He looked very handsome in his new suit, complemented by the matching dresses Avigail and I wore. The photo album and memories are a keepsake forever. My son's children already have some of his *bar mitzvah* pictures.

Avigail's *Bas Mitzvah*

Just two years later, we marked Avigail's *bas mitzvah*. I knew the affair had to be a special surprise, because we celebrated her birthday every year with a surprise party in different places with different themes.

To get her mind off the fact that her *bas mitzvah* birthday was near, I told Avigail we were going to a show. But instead, I had told all of her girlfriends to meet us at a new restaurant that had recently opened. We got into a taxi and I gave the restaurant's address. As we entered, we heard shouts of *Mazel tov! Mazel tov*! Avigail was truly surprised. We shared a delicious meal and festive dancing. The highlight of the evening came when Avigail blew out the candles on her fancy cake and opened all her presents. Everyone had a great time, the food couldn't have been better, and just like that, my little girl was a young woman according to Jewish law.

I don't know if she noticed that we never heard from her father, but if she did, she didn't mention it to me.

Chapter 15: The Children Grow Up

These were good years, the three of us together in Florida, making a happy life for ourselves. But children do grow up, and out, and we faced some important transitions.

First, Dovid graduated from *yeshiva* high school. I planned a small reception with a lavish sweet table for just before the graduation ceremony itself, which was to be held at the *shul*. Because my girlfriend lived closer to the synagogue than we did, the party was planned at her house. We invited some of our closest friends and had a delightful time. My son was regal in his new graduation suit, and smiled as his friends congratulated him and handed him gifts. My son had a close friend whose parents had not planned any kind of a celebration for him, but at the last minute his mother called and asked if they could share in our *simcha*. I got the approval of the friend whose house we were using, and we made it a mutual party which meant more people, more desserts and even more joy.

After our sweets, we all walked over to the *shul* and took our seats. The two graduates looked happy, calm and handsome. The Rabbis were sitting on the *bimah*, assembled like princes. The graduation procession began with the *rosh yeshiva* calling out the name of each graduate. As the boys walked one by one to the *bimah*, the *rosh yeshiva* read a little bit about each boy's history. The leaders of the congregation alternated with each other, giving each graduate a book from the *shul* signed by the donor.

When Dovid's name was called, he walked down the aisle with a stately stride, smiling as he passed by. I overflowed with love and pride. The Rabbi acknowledged that he had never seen Dovid without a smile, and complimented him for his various virtues and his terrific music.

After the solemn ceremony, we all assembled upstairs for a catered dinner where all the parents and teachers continued to shower the graduates with accolades.

Dovid and his friends had been accepted to universities, seminaries and *yeshivas* they had selected from all over the world. Dovid, who already knew he wanted a life of *Torah* scholarship as a Rabbi, chose an excellent *yeshiva* in Israel although, at age seventeen, he had never before been away from home for any length of time.

One of the most traumatic experiences Avigail and I ever shared (even later, when I became so ill), was watching Dovid walk up the escalator at the airport to board El Al Airlines to go to Israel the fall after his graduation to continue his rabbinical studies. Amid our tears, we felt tremendous pride. We had done all the necessary shopping, we helped him pack, we did everything but zip ourselves into his suitcases.

When he arrived in Israel, he entered the *yeshiva* and continued the link in the unbroken chain of Rabbis in our families. Avigail and I called and wrote him all the time and promptly mailed off anything he needed. We missed him terribly.

The fall and winter passed, but after *Pesach* that spring my daughter and I decided we missed Dovid too much, we were going to go to Israel. I was very eager to see for myself what kind of Rabbis, friends and under what circumstances Dovid was living. Since he never had a positive male role model to follow, I was concerned that he might choose the wrong type of person to emulate. I prayed he would come in close contact with fine Rabbis who were good teachers as well as good husbands and fathers, so he could become familiar with the way Jewish men are supposed to act. I wanted him to see wives treated with love, respect, thoughtfulness and consideration. I wanted Dovid's formative experiences to include time spent in homes where children were raised with their father's affection and attention. He was young and impressionable, so his choice of a role model would be critically important.

When our flight landed, Dovid was waiting for us. He took Avigail and me to Jerusalem to an apartment he had leased for us. When we settled down, we treated him to dinner, then we visited the *Kotel* and his *yeshiva*, which turned out to be the answer to all my prayers.

The first thing Gershon did right in his life (other than siring my two angels in the first place) was to pay for Dovid's *yeshiva* tuition and Avigail's tuition at a private Jewish school in Miami. I don't know if my ex-husband was motivated by guilt, or by the dawning recognition of what he had missed in not having a relationship with his son and daughter, or if he finally came to realize that he could well afford to support his children, but whatever his reasons, I was grateful that their education was funded.

Everything Avigail and I saw at Dovid's *yeshiva* exceeded my expectations, and we shared a great visit. I met his mentors, fine scholars and gentlemen, who truly cared about my son's well-being and education. He couldn't have been in better hands.

The next three years passed quickly. Dovid remained happy at his *yeshiva*, and he came home each year to spend *Pesach* with me and Avigail. We always put out the red carpet for him, and our home became the center of his reunions with his friends. They would pile into the old studio room and reminisce about his graduation party, their trips to and from Israel, and their occasional travels together. They changed from boys to men in front of my eyes. Thank G-d, they all became successful, married wonderful women and went on to live religious lives according to the *Torah*.

Avigail Grows Up

As Dovid studied in Israel, Abigail studied in Miami. She and I continued our life style together, going to movies and shows, eating out, sharing *Shabbosim* and holidays, and missing Dovid. We stayed busy and content.

One day during her senior year, Avigail came home earlier than usual, head down, face whiter than snow. She proceeded to tell me that her father hadn't sent the check for her tuition, so one of the Rabbis on the faculty had come into the classroom and taken her out of class. Where is the sensitivity and common sense in embarrassing a child for her father's lack of brains? Judaism teaches that humiliating someone in public is like killing. Does this kind of action help a child respect her teachers and appreciate her religion? Of course not! I was horrified.

As she cried in my arms, my heart was breaking. Avigail had never been a crier; she was always cheerful and upbeat, even during her teen years when many girls are moody. I let her release the embarrassment she felt by talking to me. I told her that the Rabbi was thoughtless and hadn't acted according to the *Torah*. As she calmed down, I explained that most Rabbis are not like that and promised to go speak with him. She sobbed as she told me that the Rabbi had said that if her tuition money didn't come in, she wouldn't get her diploma.

She had to have a diploma. She had been accepted at an excellent, prestigious seminary in New York for the coming fall, but she could not enroll without a high school diploma.

I asked Avigail to call her father's business. He was off somewhere, so I told her to get her Uncle Shlomo on the phone. I hadn't spoken to my ex-brother-in-law in years, but I told him, in a very low voice so Avigail wouldn't hear me, that if the full check for her tuition didn't arrive in twenty four hours, I would have his books subpoenaed for an audit and put a lien against his office building. I knew the company had plenty of money, despite Gershon's frequent pleas of poverty. Between Gershon's Lincoln car and Shlomo's Cadillac, they could surely afford my daughter's tuition.

The call was successful. The check arrived the next day, and I told Avigail to go back to school with her head high. I had shown my husband's family what I thought of their forgetfulness; I also wasted no time in telling the Rabbi at the school what I thought of his behavior as well.

Avigail soon forgot the incident, but I didn't. It was the only cloud in my memory a few months later as I watched her graduate.

At sixteen Avigail stood five feet seven inches tall; in my eyes, she was one of the most beautiful girls in the world, inside and out. At the ceremony, she walked down the aisle of the *shul* wearing a white robe and cap and carrying a rose, gracefully taking her seat amid her classmates. She and I both felt numb with surprise and delight when she was called to the *bimah* to receive the coveted *Novie* award, and the *rosh yeshiva* announced that she deeply deserved it. She stood smiling as her friends and their parents applauded for her, loud and clear.

Before we knew it, the ceremony was over. We enjoyed a lovely table full of desserts together with her friends and their families. Avigail's graduation class turned out to be a wonderful group of young ladies, who all went on to great success in education, marriage, motherhood, and true *Torah* lives.

Chapter 16: Illness and Recovery

Avigail and I spent a happy summer, shopping and packing, getting her ready for the seminary she would attend in the fall. As I hoped, she would make life-long friends there and have a memorable time.

Then, just as everything was going so well, I became ill for the first time in my life.

My job had always been high pressured, but I loved it. I seemed to work best under stress and deadlines; it was exhilarating. I felt productive and happy. Then, one day, as I was typing at my desk, I suddenly couldn't breathe.

The sense of panic came without warning and I had absolutely no control over my breathing or my reaction to this attack. I ran into my boss's office. She said I was hyperventilating. She sat me down and gave me a brown paper bag to breathe into, so that I could inhale concentrated oxygen, but it didn't help. I felt like I was caught in a nightmare.

Finally, she calmed me down and sent me home. I stretched out on the couch as soon as I made it through the door. Avigail was shocked to find me there when she came home, because I never gave into ailments and had deliberately given her a strong role model, even on the rare occasions when a passing cold or virus made me feel a little off.

As the evening passed, my shortness of breath subsided. We ate a light supper and I shrugged off the attack so that Avigail wouldn't worry. After all, what could she do, all alone there with me? Dovid was far away in Israel. As I began to feel like myself again, I chalked the whole thing up to menopausal changes and forgot about it.

Then, three days later at my office, it happened again. This time, I went to the doctor. He checked me out and declared that nothing was physically wrong. He said I was experiencing too much stress and prescribed tranquilizer pills, which helped alleviate the breathing episodes. When I began getting these attacks on buses or in stores, my thoughtful daughter suggested that I carry a container of water with me so that I could take a pill whenever I needed one. I fretted about the danger of becoming addicted, but they did help.

The tranquilizers gave me the illusion that the illness was under control, although it only addressed the symptoms, and I was able to continue having a normal summer. Our plans for Avigail resumed and we were delighted to learn that another Miami girl would be going to the same school. I had worried that New York would be cold and lonely for my child, who had never been away from me before.

When we flew to New York, I had an attack. I had to take one of my pills and the stewardess had to walk me up and down the aisle on the plane. I was feeling okay by the time we landed, and we got in a cab and headed for the seminary in Brooklyn.

Avigail had a pretty room and the other girls and the housemother seemed very cordial. We unpacked, made up her bed and hung her clothes in the closet. Then we went out to eat.

That afternoon, we checked into a local kosher hotel for a day and night together before school started. I had forgotten what it was like to be chilly and we had a ball taking the subway to Manhattan and buying Avigail coats, gloves, boots and winter scarves. We rambled up and down Fifth Avenue, finding bargains at Bloomingdales, before we boarded the subway back to Brooklyn.

I felt another attack coming on as we got off the subway and, since I had no water with me, found myself in a bar yelling for a drink of water. I thought that was pretty comical for an Orthodox woman and tried to focus Avigail's thoughts on the silliness of the bar scene rather than the persistence of my illness.

We picked up a barbecued chicken at a kosher restaurant we passed and took it back to the hotel where we spent a delightful evening with our feet propped up, watching TV and eating chicken like two ladies of leisure.

It was very traumatic for both of us to say good-bye to each other the next day. We had a luxurious room service breakfast and I walked Avigail back to the seminary. Our parting tears and hugs were heart-rending, but I reassured her and explained that she would soon be having a wonderful time. I promised to call her everyday and fly her home for the *High Holidays*. I got in a taxi, leaving her in the arms of her housemother, surrounded by new friends. I felt very proud of my daughter.

My trip home was uneventful and when I called Avigail that evening, she sounded happy and reported that a few local girls had already invited her to their homes for *Shabbos.*

My happiness was complete when Dovid called from Israel the next day. He was delighted that Avigail was settled in such a good seminary, and that they would soon be living close to each other. His three years in Israel were almost concluded and he was planning to continue his studies in New York City.

I felt wonderful knowing that my children would have each other at hand, although I wasn't so pleased that their education in New York meant that Gershon was back in their lives. Avigail called me after her first week of seminary and told me her father visited her often. She asked how I had ever married such a man. I told her I wasn't sure myself, but urged her to be polite to her father and to have a free conscience about accepting any financial help he was willing to extend.

I told Dovid the same thing when he arrived in New York City; let your father provide you with new clothes and nice meals, and save your own money. I figured my children were entitled.

I eventually figured it out. My weak-willed ex-husband was trying to clear his conscience and trying to repent for neglecting his children during the most important years of their lives. This was an impossible task, especially since his Oedipal obsession with his mother continued. He tried to evoke pity from them for his depression and helplessness. Fortunately, my children had become immune to his nonsense. They had been away from him too long to become his victims now. As they settled into life in New York City, I had other things to worry about in Florida. My health quickly deteriorated as my breathing problems escalated. I went from episode to episode.

My breathing got very bad one Sunday. I was straightening up my house and got an attack of breathlessness that left me gasping and helpless. I tried to rest, I tried to breathe, I even tried using a paper bag again. I started to cry, and that must have helped, because I caught my breath. While I had some control, I phoned a female doctor from my office's medical staff, hoping another woman might be more aware of what to do, since I still thought this problem was related to menopause.

She was playing golf and when she called me back, she was annoyed to have been paged. She declared, "You're just hyperventilating. Go see a psychiatrist."

I ran to the phone book and found a psychiatrist in the neighborhood who was home and was willing to meet me at his office. I was distraught, in tears and nearly breathless again by the time I got there. He asked me a few questions and prescribed another tranquilizer at a higher dosage than my old ones.

I filled the prescription, took a pill and slept through the night, but I couldn't put any credence in what he had told me. He blamed my attacks on anxiety brought on by my children leaving me. I thought that was ridiculous; I had urged them to go, to get their education and begin their adult lives. I had a full life without them, after all these years of dependence, and I resented this stranger trying to instantly analyze matters he knew nothing about.

The pills helped for a while, but I never felt compatible with the psychiatrist. I had a complete physical and checked out normally, although no one thought to test me for chemical imbalance. My menstruation had stopped completely by now and, although I never got hot flashes, I still figured the change of life had affected my breathing.

When I told the psychiatrist he wasn't helping me, he threw me out of his office saying that he liked his patients to be happy and smiling. My continued illness must have injured his ego. I found another physician, a warm, caring man, on my office's medical roster and put myself under his care. He agreed that menopause caused my symptoms and continued the tranquilizers. Unfortunately, the episodes of gasping for breath continued and I realized I was frequently disturbing my colleagues when I struggled to breathe.

Avigail came home for the holidays and I concealed as much of my illness from her as I could. I took my pills and carried out my usual tasks, although they seemed far more tiring and difficult than usual. I did not want to send her back to New York City with any unnecessary worries that might interfere with her studies.

After she left, I worked with a psychologist who taught me breathing exercises, but that didn't help either. I returned to the office unable to function because I had to take more and more tranquilizers to maintain the ability to breathe. It became increasingly difficult to work, and it was harder and harder for my co-workers to contend with my coughing, crying and apologizing. I was caught in a dreadful spiral, and finally decided to resign. I found it very difficult to leave the best job, and the best boss I had ever had, but I didn't think I had any choice.

I had accrued about two thousand dollars in benefits and I promptly applied for social security and disability payments.

The illness took a terrible toll. I started to borrow money from friends. I became afraid to leave my home in fear of having an attack, and developed agoraphobia. I popped pills every time I had to grocery shop and spent most of my time in bed, the only place I felt well and safe. I tried a special health-oriented diet on a friend's advice, and I lost weight, but I didn't feel any better.

My doctor advised me over the phone and kept prescribing tranquilizers, which the pharmacy delivered. I was turned down twice for Medicare, before I was finally accepted. My days became bad dreams, one after the other. The only saving grace was that I got a part-time job, making fundraising phone calls at home, so I had a little income again. Finally, my doctor said he could no longer help me and told me to see a well-known neuroscientist.

I was offended at first. I thought such a referral meant I was crazy. I protested that I didn't need a brain doctor, but I soon discovered that my protests were based on ignorance. The doctor must have been a messenger from G-d because he sent me to an angel, and at last I got some real help.

The neurologist saw me and took my medical history. As we spoke, I had to stretch out on his floor to try to catch my breath. He said he hadn't seen a case like mine, and urged me to check into the hospital immediately. Because I had no insurance, I asked him to handle me on an outpatient basis. He agreed reluctantly, but said I couldn't handle medication any stronger than my current prescription. I suffered through the next few days as he made a "brain map" and, at last, arrived at the diagnosis that gave me a direction to pursue. He said I had panic attacks based on stress, pressure and depression, due to a chemical imbalance.

I set out to cure myself, and found that an accumulation of all the medications I had been taking was having additional ill effects on me, including sleeplessness, nausea, excess toxicity and headaches. I tried everything I could, and received some assurance from learning that I had lived such a high-stress lifestyle that menopause, which many women handle easily, had been very difficult for my enervated body. But my symptoms continued and even my wonderful new physician didn't know what to do for me.

At last, a friend called Avigail and told her to come home because I shouldn't be alone. I resisted, I didn't want to do that to my daughter, but I was in very bad shape. I found it difficult to even make a bed. Avigail came home and was a true angel in every way. I felt terribly guilty about disrupting her life, but I finally got into therapy and the therapist assured me that children are resilient and that Avigail would be fine as soon as I recovered.

I was hospitalized in November, thanks to a loan from my daughter that made it possible for the hospital to admit me. Avigail took a job, visited me daily, including *Shabbos*, and had friends spend nights with her in the apartment. Her brother came to keep her company for a while. At last I was released, with new medication and a weekly therapy schedule.

I still felt awful, but Avigail and I got some good news, news that made me want to be well again. Dovid called and told us he was getting married.

We immersed ourselves in wedding plans: shopping, selecting chantilly lace for Avigail's dress and arranging for it to be made, and preparing for all the festivities. Yet as we went about these delightful activities, I felt increasingly depressed, weak and ill.

At last, Avigail insisted that we visit the doctor again together. I agreed. I wanted to live, to love life again, to relish my son's wedding. We sat in the doctor's office and he began to read off a list of all the medications he had prescribed for me. As he called out one particular drug, my daughter stopped him.

"My mother never took that," she said.

Thank G-d for my daughter. "I wonder why she missed it. It's very important. I have never seen anyone suffer like her," the doctor said, writing a prescription for it and handing me a dose right there in his office.

Within minutes of the medication taking effect, I began to feel like my old self again. I hugged and kissed my daughter. By the end of the week I realized that I was finally on the long road to recovery, although I still needed weekly therapy and I couldn't handle any stress.

The medicine turned out to be so effective that, thank G-d, I improved steadily. The panic attacks subsided; my breathing became reliable again. I even overheard Avigail telling Gershon on the phone that it was good to have Mommy back again.

I breezed through my house, cleaning it up the way I liked it. I had it painted and reupholstered the furniture for a more up-to-date look. I continued my home fundraising business and kept taking the miracle medicine. I learned it had not been developed for psychiatric patients, but for epileptics who were depressed. It made them feel happy again. The use of it for a patient suffering stress-related panic attacks was new and, much to my relief, it worked. As I recovered enough to enjoy a pre-wedding visit from Dovid to begin discussing the wedding parties and plans, I changed my long time message to Avigail. "Don't try to be a superwoman," I urged her. "It takes a terrible toll on your health. Do whatever you have to do to stay well. Hire help. Use your energy for what really matters, like raising children."

Today, she is the happy mother of three cute little boys. Her home, like mine, is spotless, and much to my gratification, she has household help twice a week. But I am getting ahead of my story.

First, I got well. Then my children got married.

Chapter 17: Mother of the Groom; Mother of the Bride

When Dovid visited me during my recovery, I realized that I needed to focus some of my energy on meeting my son's future in-laws. I still wasn't strong enough for long conversations with people I didn't know. I was advised just to start the conversation, be cordial, listen, and let them continue. I didn't have money for the gifts I would have loved to have given them when we first met, but I made it up to them later.

At last, Avigail and I flew to New York. Dovid met us at the airport. By the smile on his face and the look in his eye, I knew G-d had answered my prayers and sent him the love of his life, a young woman who is beautiful, inside and out.

I met my future *machatonim* and followed my therapist's advice. Despite my convalescent fears, the conversation went very well. I was so relieved when Dovid told me they were impressed; so was I.

✡✡✡

Before the *chuppah*, I stole a few quiet moments with my son. There was so much to say during those brief, emotional minutes together, and so little time to say it.

On impulse, I asked him what the most memorable moment of his Florida childhood had been. He was silent a moment, and nostalgically said, "the wonderful *oneg Shabbos* you made for my friends and my counselor." I remembered it instantly. A beautiful *Shabbos* gathering where the counselor told stirring stories, the boys sang and played games and ate to their heart's content. Their mothers called me and said their sons couldn't stop talking about the amount of food I had served. It was a spiritual *Shabbos* and a feast. Dovid and I laughed and talked a few more minutes before I sneaked a kiss on his cheek and left him.

I saw him a while later when I was called to the *choson's tish*, where the Rabbis were preparing Dovid for the signing of the *tenayim* (engagement contract) and the *ketubah* (marriage contract). My *machataineste* and I simultaneously, joyfully, broke the ritual plate. I went back to the room where Avigail was dressing. She looked stunning to me, but then she always did. Then the bride's mother and I walked the *kallah* to the draped and decorated *kallah's* chair to receive the traditional *mazel tov* from our friends and family.

"I survived, I survived," ran the refrain in my mind, as I sat watching, my son walking forward with Gershon and his future father-in-law to *badek* his charming *kallah*. I looked at Dovid, and at my beautiful Avigail, and felt that all my struggles, abuse, and illness had meant something because they brought me to this moment.

I quickly took a peek at Avigail's face and said a special prayer to G-d to send her someone extra special who would appreciate all her *midos*. I couldn't imagine how I could ever repay her for all the trouble I caused her during the most traumatic time of my life. I heard my therapist's voice reassuring me, "If you are well, all will be well with your daughter."

The sound of festive music brought me back to the present, to the joyful *simcha* I had thought I would be too ill to attend. The traditional, moving Hebrew melodies were accompanied by clapping and singing as all the men attending the wedding danced nearer to the *kallah's* chair. Ah, I thought for a minute, what happened to the eight-year-old who held onto my skirt when we got off the train in Miami so long ago? Hundreds of Dovid's *yeshiva* friends and guests sang, and danced, and clapped, as they escorted him as he fulfilled one of the most meaningful ancient biblical rituals, *badeking* the bride, covering the bride's face with her veil before the wedding ceremony.

As tears filled my eyes, I saw that Avigail was crying, too. I blinked away tears of joy, mental images of a *bris*, a *pidyon haben*, a *bar mitzvah*, a young man getting on to an airplane on his way to *yeshiva* in Israel for continued *Torah* learning, and saw before me my handsome son taking his precious *kallah's* white veil gently in his hands and covering her shining, loving face. She looked up toward my son and I witnessed the innocent, pure love in her eyes, a love reflected on Dovid's face. I knew then, with great contentment, that my son would be a loyal, strong and supportive husband to her, the husband I had prepared him to be, not the husband his father had been. My son would "leave" me and cleave to his wife, as he should.

I managed to walk down the aisle for the wedding ceremony and dance with my lovely daughter-in-law and my lovely daughter. The wedding was a magical evening, and I felt such an encompassing sense of celebration and blessing.

As I was standing under the *chuppah*, I looked at my beloved son and thought, "before me stands a king," as I walked around him seven times, following the bride in her magnificent gown. I listened as the Rabbi read the seven blessings and the *ketubah*, and rejoiced at the shouted *mazel tovs!* as Dovid broke the ritual wine glass. I smiled and decided that I could pat myself on the back, just for a moment; I knew I'd done a good job.

I kissed my son and my new daughter-in-law, who were immediately escorted to the privacy of the *yichud* room, and I started to enjoy the entire *simcha*, the meal, the blessings, the dancing, the joy that G-d had allowed me to witness.

By the time I got back to my hotel room, my head was spinning. I was so excited, so elated, so exhilarated, that even after I got into bed, I couldn't sleep.

That night G-d sent me my mission, to seriously develop the idea I was toying with years before, of writing this book. It came to me as I lay there, awake and overjoyed. I knew I could use my years of suffering to help other women. I knew I could reach out to my sisters in the Orthodox community who were trapped in abusive, loveless marriages. I had been given the great *mitzvah* of being able to help. Now I knew what I had to do.

✡✡✡

I went to one of the *sheva brochos* for the newly-weds before I headed back to Miami to preserve my fragile health, and to prepare for *Pesach.* When friends invited me to spend the holiday with them at a hotel, I accepted gratefully. I checked in with my doctor after one mild attack of lightheadedness and he told me to watch my blood sugar levels and to cut back on my medication. I felt I was really making progress. And I was doing fine on my own again.

Avigail stayed in New York City to resume her studies at the seminary, picking up the pieces of her life now that she no longer had to nurse me.

Gershon's life in New York had changed dramatically. A year before Dovid's wedding, Hodel had died. Gershon took it very hard. In his eyes, in the everlasting throes of his sickness which even death could not cure, his mother was a saint who was placed above and beyond anyone else. After he sat *shiva* for Hodel, Gershon told Dovid and Avigail something along the lines of, "I have nothing to live for now." My gentle children only said, "But Daddy, you have us." He apologized profusely, but they both had long since come to understand their father's obsession. To their credit, they tried to rebuild a relationship with him. After the wedding, Avigail, Dovid and his bride even spent *Pesach* in the mountains with Gershon.

✡✡✡

Months later, as I sat in my Miami apartment one evening, grateful to be well and busy, the phone rang. It was Avigail with the news she and I had long awaited: she was getting married.

I already liked her future husband. I had met him when he came to Florida to take Avigail out. He was a special person with all the *midos* I had taught her to seek in a future mate, someone who emulated the brother she admired and not the father who had ignored her.

Avigail called me from New York the moment they got engaged and I met my future *machatonim* over the telephone, wonderful people.

Soon, I joined my daughter in New York for a wild shopping spree and we had a ball. I bought her everything for her new home, from soup to nuts, and outfitted her with all the clothes a new wife could need. Even today, Avigail teases me that I bought her enough bridal clothes to last a lifetime.

As the wedding drew closer, we went back and forth from Miami to New York. I held a *kiddush* on *Succos* in her honor at our synagogue in Miami, and I also hosted an engagement party, complete with orchestra and photographer, for all her friends and the children for whom she once baby-sat. We chose invitations and a glorious wedding dress (which, as was customary at that time, we rented). I froze, stunned with admiration and delight, when I saw how stately and magnificent my baby looked when she tried on the gown. For a split second I had a flashback of a gorgeous little girl getting off the train in Florida, holding onto the other side of my dress, and together with her mother and brother was looking forward to a new life in the sunny south.

Back in New York City, I found the gifts I wanted for my future son-in-law and his parents. They are lovely people and we get along beautifully. (By the way, that's also true of my son's in-laws).

Gershon took over the job of inviting all the guests and he footed the whole bill for the wedding. I left the headaches to him and he finally took on some of the responsibility he had always managed to shirk. I will admit that I resented seeing him share in Avigail's *simcha*. He never took an interest in her as a child, but that was water under the bridge. He did underwrite a beautiful wedding even if it was because of a nagging guilty conscience. I came as a guest and enjoyed every fabulous minute.

When I had a second with her before the ceremony, I asked my daughter the same question I had asked my son at that moment, what did she remember most fondly about growing up in Florida? After thinking a while, she said everything was fun and memorable, even food shopping. We reminisced about our trips to Israel and other vacations, all the movies and plays we saw, all the surprise birthday parties we enjoyed, the hotel shows we liked, even her high school graduation.

The wedding was a joyous *simcha*, with wonderful food and music, and joy on every face. Avigail's *badecken* was very emotional. She and her *choson* were obviously so connected, so right for each other, thank G-d. Avigail was regal as we walked to the *chuppah*. Standing beside her, I felt confident that my angel was in the best hands. I still remember the first dance I had with her after she and her new husband came into the ballroom and were introduced as man and wife. It was emotional and momentous; the music, the guests, the delightful sense of joy and celebration seemed heaven sent.

I left my married daughter in the hands of her husband with a great feeling of peaceful tranquillity. I felt confident they were entering a marriage of love and happiness (for one hundred and twenty years!). I couldn't help smiling as I thanked G-d for a child who never had anything but a smile on her face, who never gave me a minute of trouble from the day she was born, who was a joy to be with from morning to evening.

✧✧✧

Today I take tremendous joy and *naches* from my son's and daughter's families, my darling grandchildren, and my in-laws and our entire extended family. They are all thriving, building busy and productive *Torah* lives.

Dovid is a wonderful helpful husband, terrific father, breadwinner and scholar. Avigail is an excellent housekeeper, gourmet cook, and devoted wife and mother of three wonderful boys. She sets a table and entertains better than I ever did, and when I am seated at her table, my happiness has no bounds.

I am so proud of both of them and their families; they are all any mother or grandmother could ever want. Thank G-d.

Chapter 18: The Orthodox Abuse Center

My book is written; it is in your hands. What would you have done if you were in my place? My next goal is to open an abuse shelter for Orthodox women who need a haven where they can begin to rebuild their lives. So far, the shelter is only a dream. But already, I can begin counseling women who share the suffering I experienced. The nominal fee I plan to charge for counseling will help build the shelter and cover my mailing and phone expenses.

One day, an eight hundred number will be all that an abused Orthodox wife will need. I hope to create a place where a woman can call and, under the immediate sponsorship of the Center, board a plane and come with her children to a safe haven without spending a penny.

I had nowhere to run with my young children. I was literally trapped and alone in the world with an abusive, ill husband. I had to bide my time, hoard my pennies and plan my exodus carefully, so I well understand the importance of an Orthodox Abuse Center.

The Orthodox woman, especially the Orthodox mother, has special religious obligations, needs and commitments to fulfill to insure the continuance of our heritage. Therefore, a center must provide a special environment to fulfill these needs:

- a strictly kosher kitchen
- *yeshivas* (one for boys, one for girls) for the children
- a *Shabbos* and *yom tov* atmosphere
- an Orthodox synagogue where boys over thirteen

can *daven* with a *minyan* and where younger boys can sit with men who provide good role models for learning.

The shelter will also have:

- a beautiful play room for the children
- a good library and reading room
- a beauty shop (a big help in building self-esteem)
- attractive bedrooms and home-like dining and living areas
- a swimming pool, exercise and entertainment facilities

An Orthodox woman can make a better social adjustment in the company of other Orthodox women. But a woman fleeing from abuse will not only need companionship. She'll also need a peaceful environment providing emotional and mental stability, so that she can rebuild her self-esteem and begin to envision a positive future for herself and her children.

In a homey atmosphere, the shelter can help women address the dangerous stress and pressure that can ruin healthy bodies. I envision a place decorated like a cheerful home.

But I also envision a shelter that offers top-notch professional services, such as:

- Orthodox social workers on staff
- Orthodox therapists on staff
- Orthodox physicians, attorneys, psychologists, Rabbis, and psychiatrists on call.
- Excellent security, so that abusive men cannot endanger wives who are in residence
- Job training programs for those who need workforce skills.

The purpose of the Orthodox Abuse Center is to help women begin new lives, to instill in them renewed self-respect and direction so they can function productively. Our goal is to reunite the family if possible, and to try to find out the reason for this abuse, a problem which never filtered into Orthodox Jewish families before.

A first step will be to enable these women to contribute to their own upkeep by carrying out services the center will need, from cooking, to cleaning, sewing, teaching and more. They will need to feel they can make a contribution and be proud of themselves. They will benefit from being busy and from being loved.

If you would like to contribute to making the shelter a reality, please write to me care of the publisher.

Chapter 19: Reflections

I want to take a moment here to reflect upon some of the disparate things I have learned on the long road to independent happy living. We need to discuss how marriages are arranged, how mental illness, particularly the Oedipus Complex, because that is the mental illness I had to cope with, can affect a family, and what my experiences have taught me about being a good mother, grandmother and, oh yes, a very good mother-in-law.

The *Shidduch*

We do our children a grave injustice when we allow untruths or misplaced values to permeate the institution of the *shidduch*, the introduction of a boy and girl to each other for the purpose of matrimony.

When those involved feel it is okay to lie, marriages begin based on false premises. Virtues are exaggerated; shortcomings are concealed.

When the time comes for you to be involved in a *shidduch*, consider the innocent victims if you lie, who will have the final cry of pain, suffering and anguish if a marriage ends; no one but our beloved, precious children.

Parents must search for spouses of good *midos* for their children, partners of kindness, good character, warmth, love, sincerity; do not settle for anything less. Your daughter deserves a husband who is an honest worker or a serious learner, a person of good reputation. If you feel that someone doesn't measure up, don't give in to the emotions of the moment.

My experience would lead me to be particularly cautious about a candidate who is excessively attached to his or her parents or extended family. I would reject a potential mate who was insulting or impolite. Lack of respect and lack of feeling are danger signals. Check out any problems thoroughly in advance. If a boy is too possessive or angers easily, that's a warning. If he pushes you, blames you for his inadequacies or, heaven forbid, pinches or hits you, get rid of him immediately. Before the *shidduch* is the time for someone who knows there is a problem to speak out, to warn the girl's parents; of course, we should avoid *loshen hora*, but not at the expense of failing to tell the truth in time to save a young girl's future.

I would tell young girls, that as much as I respect and cherish learning, don't select a husband just because he is a *talmid chochom* (he could also be a *talmid teepash*). You don't want to marry a book; you want to marry a person who will love and cherish you, and put you first, as the *Torah* commands. The young man who will respect you, help you with the children, lead his family as your partner, and carry his fair share of home responsibility is the husband you want.

Both boys and girls should choose their professions with care. Don't go into a field just because it is what your parents want or what your peers respect. Set yourself up to lead a constructive life by gaining skills in a profession that truly interests you; don't worry about what other people think. You can make a living thousands of respectable ways.

I urge girls not to rush into marriage. Stay single until you have a source of income, a *parnossa* of your own, so you can respect yourself and, if necessary G-d forbid, fend for yourself in the world.

I would tell girls, nothing is wrong with getting married after you finish seminary or college. From ages eighteen to twenty, your tastes will change as you mature from teen-hood to womanhood. A twenty two year-old will understand that the moody, smoldering, mysteriously silent man who might seem romantic to a teenager will make an unloving, surly husband.

I would tell both boys and girls, look for personality and character in a mate; they wear a lot better than good looks or social status. Take your time. This is the most important decision of your life. Don't hurry. If you make the wrong choice, you will regret it for a very long time.

The Bad Mother: Oedipus Redux

The poison of abuse and divorce are seeping into our community. Today, women are being publicly embarrassed or insulted by husbands who take out their inadequacies and inferiority on them. Women are controlled by husbands who injure them, emotionally or even physically. Never doubt that emotional, mental and psychological abuse can be just as devastating as physical or sexual abuse.

I know because I survived emotional, mental and psychological abuse. Gershon never raised his hand to me; he didn't have to. His neglect and distance, his lack of intimacy and caring, his critical nastiness, his sick attachment to his mother to the exclusion of all others, were abuse enough.

I bided my time until my children were of an age to leave. I could handle his illness by ignoring him, but I didn't want my children exposed to it.

The only way to save a marriage where physical abuse has occurred is to leave at the first instance and seek prompt counseling. Some abusers can be helped, some cannot. The habit of physical abuse comes from having been abused as a child, or having seen abuse in the home from a timid father and an overbearing mother. It is insidious and very dangerous.

The emotional abuse I suffered was caused by an Oedipus Complex, a man's unhealthy attachment to his mother, named after the mythological Greek figure Oedipus, who married his mother after killing his competition, his father.

From my reading and studying (and I have had this passage reviewed by a psychologist), I have learned that the mother of the Oedipus victim, in addition to being a very selfish, unhealthy person, has within herself an emotional void for love she never received from her husband. She trains her sons from the cradle to serve her, whether deliberately or inadvertently, motivated by her own pathos and depression. I wish we could teach our children when they are small and are learning the fifth commandment that parents are to be respected but are not allowed to destroy the *shalom bayis* in their grown children's homes.

The domineering mother takes full advantage of the fifth commandment. She demands more than honor: she is a dictator who instills guilt in her children. She is sure no one knows anything but her, and so she tells her sons. Day in and day out, they are taught that they are ignorant and weak while she is all-knowing and strong. Eventually they lose the spirit and strength to fight back, particularly when this domination is accompanied by slaps, yelling and insults. The resulting man vacillates, ignores problems, has no independent direction, and cannot make decisions for himself, because every decision has always been made for him. He has a deep inferiority complex and usually low self esteem.

When her children are small, this disturbed mother stops them short when they speak, embarrasses them in public, and punishes them if they voice an opinion that doesn't mirror hers. She instills a sense of inferiority in her children by withholding praise and being perpetually superior, covering up her own low self esteem.

Often, these domineering, destructive women have timid,

or absent husbands who don't care what their wives do as long as they don't have to be bothered by it. They pay no attention to their wives and little to their children, and as a result they offer no alternative role model for their sons, or their daughters.

The children's minds are destroyed, they receive no emotional support, and all the love the mother projects is self-love, not maternal love.

In the case of Hodel, she was also vain about her looks and dress, without any reason to be so. She was a bad housekeeper but criticized other women's housekeeping. She had few friends, notably few women friends, and she hated other women. Hodel was envious, embittered and jealous. Gershon and Shlomo received affection from her only when they evoked her pity. She never kissed them or her husband, whom she hypocritically mothered and catered to verbally while dominating him in every other way. I don't know if these behaviors are part of the classic Oedipus Complex, but they sure did a thorough job of ruining my husband. He was always quick to say "I can't" to responsibility while running to his mother.

By the time we married, I was walking into a strange situation too far gone for anyone to cure. Gershon did not need a wife; he had no sexual drive and his only love affair was with his mother. Like most men with an Oedipus Complex, he knew he had a illness, but he dealt with by remaining silent about it. Once or twice in his life, he admitted to an obsession with his mother, while simultaneously acknowledging that he had neither the willingness nor the ability to change it.

I wondered if the Oedipus man really loves his mother, or if he hates her so completely that he takes out enormous frustration and hatred on his wife, to avoid confronting his mother for fear of what she would do to him.

I wondered if the mother of an Oedipus man instigates discord in his home to boost her own position with him because she is jealously unable to share her son.

I found this kind of behavior incomprehensible at the time. Hodel would tell Gershon, "Your wife looks terrible in that coat. She should look the way I do in mine. She's not beautiful, I used to be more beautiful than that when I was her age." He would repeat and believe her comments. This kind of comment was not occasional, it was constant. When someone would praise me, she would contradict them. Her conversation was always focused on putting people down, constantly, about everything. A good word never came from her mouth or his.

Gershon rarely responded to Hodel's diatribes; he learned better as a little boy. He was speechless and confused in the face of her power. Gershon always felt guilt about his mother. He felt guilty if he didn't call her often during the day, if he didn't visit her every time he entered or exited his own home, if he didn't fulfill her every demand, no matter how unreasonable, although he could easily pass a day or more without concern for his wife and children. If he ignored her for five minutes, she came banging at my door asking why he wasn't with her.

Hodel had other problems. Her mother died in childbirth, so she felt abandoned, I believe, and therefore came to hate all other women. Her son was distant to men. She was burdened by terrible guilt because she refused to take in her brother's children during the Holocaust. She wrote to him that she could not take his children because she could barely feed her own, and his children perished. I think that is why she couldn't stand to see me show affection for my children; her guilt was just too overwhelming. She always found fault when I kissed and hugged my children and she never showed any affection for her own sons.

I did not let her dominate me, so she hated me all the more. Nonetheless, she got what she wanted. I gave her back her damaged son, who wasn't worth fighting for. She took full advantage, going out with him every night, holding his hand as they walked down the street, acting with him the way a young, flirtatious girl does with a date.

The hate my mother-in-law had for me backfired on both her and Gershon. In fact, her hatred for me almost killed the son she was supposed to love. After my divorce, intending to keep the family business (which had been built by Gershon) away from me, Hodel bequeathed eighty percent of it to Shlomo, who was still married to Lana, and twenty percent to Gershon. She died before either of her sons, and when Shlomo died, (he was not divorced), fifty percent of his holdings went to Lana. My children lost their *yerusha* to my nephews, who threatened to go to court. We are talking about *b'nei Torah* whom I helped bring up. The salvation for Dovid and Avigail may come from the *Din Torah*, but it is iffy. The lesson is, hatred destroys. Innocent people can be caught up in this disease. Families get torn apart.

Family unity, *shalom bayis*, is a basic Judaic value, but Hodel never developed a *Torah* based value system. She had her own *shulchan aruch*. She felt good if she had a nicer dress than someone else, and often left me to feed her nephews and Shlomo while she shopped for *shmatte* after *shmatte*.

She needed to foster dependence, not independence, in her children to feed her own needs. And it worked. Gershon was terribly over dependent on her, a symptom that went unnoticed, or seemed like an asset, when we were dating and engaged. The old saying, "If a man is good to his mother, he'll be good to his wife," only applies to normal people, not to unhealthy situations like this. In fact, the primary stress that can push an Oedipal man to a nervous breakdown is to be caught between two strong, domineering women: his mother and his wife.

Gershon was spared this because I left. I refused to fight, to expose my children to this, or to allow him to remain before their eyes as a model of adult behavior. A friend of Gershon's told him to go for counseling, but Gershon answered, "Why should I go.

He'll tell me to leave my mother, and I don't want to do that."

I had to leave for the sake of Avigail and Dovid. I wanted them to learn from our friends how a husband and wife carry out their roles in a normal family. In Florida, my children had friends and a home filled with *shalom bayis*. All they could find in their father's home was depression, criticism and sadness, no humor, no light.

Psychiatric treatment does exist for a man with a Oedipus Complex, but it is very intensive and involves many long visits. The man also must be willing to cooperate. Treatment includes building up his self-esteem and independence and creating a physical separation from his mother. But first, he has to want to change, and Gershon never did.

The Torah View

Our *Torah* is very clear about how men should treat women. The *Torah* is adamantly against rape and sexual abuse. One of the *Torah's* most difficult and sacred laws deals with family purity (*taharas hamishpocho*), which leads to family harmony, the basis of a secure, joyful marriage.

The *Torah* is very concerned with a mutually-gratifying sexual relationship in a marriage. How wise the *Torah* is, and how wise our sages were, to provide laws leading to family happiness. We are instructed to institute a monthly physical separation (at least twelve days) until the woman submerges her entire body in the *mikvah*, the spiritual ritual bath. Only then is the woman's husband allowed to touch her. This monthly separation is not only a restriction on "instant gratification," but it teaches couples *Hashem's* purpose in having a passionate and spiritual reunion.

In a normal, loving marriage this separation revives the excitement and desires of physical lovemaking between the partners. Each partner waits for the other, like the groom waits for his bride and the bride waits for her groom.

This *mitzvah* is founded on a man's duty to satisfy and gratify his wife sexually. How lucky a husband is who puts his wife's gratification first and gives himself wholly to her. In turn, he will receive many rewards, including a loving helpmate and personal gratification in his lovemaking.

On the other hand, a man only creates misfortune for himself if he sins against his wife. This includes verbally insulting or embarrassing her and then demanding that she give herself to him sexually. This mistreatment of a wife is definitely against the *Torah* viewpoint. The marriage contract does not justify harassment or mistreatment. A husband is never allowed to force himself on his wife.

According to our holy *Torah*, a couple's sexual relations should come within the framework and environment of peace, mutual desire and mutual respect for one another. At its highest, the marital act of love-making is the union of two *neshamas*, a holy union to be revered and respected.

Being The Best I Can Be

My job now is to be the best mother, grandmother and mother-in-law I can be, and to grow older gracefully, but not old. I have learned from what I have experienced, and I work very hard now to do the right things. I know my children are proud of me. I am, thank G-d, self-sufficient. It is my pleasure to give to my children and grandchildren and not to take from them. As a grandmother, it is my joy and *naches* to play with my grandchildren, to kiss and love and spoil them, but it is not my place to raise them; that is their parents' job.

As a grandmother, I believe in letting the parents make the rules. I respect their wishes, whether I agree with them or not, and uphold their restrictions with the children. I ask permission from them before I make plans with the children. I am careful to avoid any arguments, even if they ask my opinion, and I tell them I don't wish to get involved.

If I was writing rules for grandmas and mothers-in-law, I'd write "**MIND YOUR OWN BUSINESS**" as the first rule. It is not your affair what your daughter-in-law makes for dinner or how she tends her home. Your son-in-law's work or hobbies are not your concern. Be neutral when it comes to your children's affairs. Keep busy with your own life. Have a full life which includes lots of friends. Maintain your interests and your own social agenda. If you are asked to baby-sit, grab the opportunity to spend time with the precious little ones and to help your grown children.

The best way to maintain a good relationship is to put a piece of tape over your mouth. Even with a daughter, you must be discrete about criticizing.

The hardest part is aging gracefully, without becoming querulous or demanding. Act your age and dress your age, and stay as well as you can. I know my children will take care of me, but I don't want them to have to do it. I refuse to burden them. They have their own responsibilities.

Chapter 20: In Conclusion

I don't regret a thing I did. The force that kept me going all my life is my deep faith and strong belief in G-d. I instilled this faith in my children and they, in turn, are instilling it in their children. While I thank G-d I am independent and busy and do not have to depend on my children, they know they can rely on me. I am always there for them; they and their children are my *naches*.

I wish you all health, happiness, success, and continued *naches* from your children and grandchildren, and we should all be *zocheh* to witness the coming of M*oshiach bimhayra v'yuomanoo*.

Glossary

abba - father

afikomen - a piece of matzah ceremonially hidden by the children and used as a bargaining tool for gifts before returning it to the host at the *seder*.

al pi halacha - according to Jewish law

badek(en) - the veiling of the bride

bar mitzvah - a thirteen year old boy is obligated as a man according to Jewish law and can be counted in a ***minyan***

bashert - as it is supposed to be, ordained by G-d

bas mitzvah - a twelve year old girl is obligated as a woman according to Jewish law

ben Torah - brilliant ***Torah*** student

bimah - the podium in the synagogue where the ***Torah*** is read

bimhara v'yamanu - hastily, in our time

bitochon - deep faith and trust

b'nei Torah - educated, learned men

bris - circumcision performed by a ***mohel***

choson - engaged man, groom

choson's tish - groom's table where he welcomes guests and signs the ***tenayim***

chinuch - education (also, dedication)

chometz - bread or leavened flour, not allowed during ***Pesach***

chosid shoteh - a superficially learned man who is also a fool

chuppah - wedding canopy

daven - pray

derech eretz - respect

Din Torah - Jewish court of law

ema - mother

emunah - faith

esrog - citrus fruit used during *Succos*

ezer - helpmate

frum - Jewishly observant

get - religious certificate of divorce

haftorah- the section from Prophets or other holy writings read on *Shabbos* and holidays after the *Torah* portion

hakofos- circular processions with Torah scrolls

hamentashen -- three-cornered pastry made for *Purim*

Hashem - G-d, literally "The Name"

ish- man

isha- woman

kallah - engaged woman, bride

ketubah - marriage contract

kiruv - outreach; return to orthodoxy

K'lal Yisrael - People of Israel

knegdo - against; if a woman feels emotionally, mentally or physically threatened by her husband, she turns into his most bitter enemy

kollel- a community where husbands study post graduate theological studies while wives often work to support them; married students

Kotel - the holy Western Wall in Jerusalem

loshen hora - gossip, insults, literally "evil talk"

lulav - palm branches used at *Succos*

machataineste- mother of the daughter-in-law or son- in- law

machatoonim - your child's in-laws

mazel tov - congratulations

mechazek- strengthen

Megillah - the Book of Esther, read at *Purim*

midos - character

minyan - group of 10 men (quorum) necessary for public prayer

mikvah - ritual bath

mispallel - pray

mitzvah - good deed, *Torah* commandment

mitzvah girl - a girl or woman who tries to do good deeds

mohel - a person learned in Jewish law who is qualified to perform circumcisions

moshiach- messiah

motzie- benediction over bread

naches - joyful pride

neshama - soul

novi - prophet

oneg Shabbos - enjoying the *Sabbath* with friends, and with food and drink

parnossa - financial income, able to be self-supporting

Pesach- Passover holiday

pidyon haben - redemption of the first born

Rabbonim -Rabbis

seder - *Pesach* meal where the *Exodus* saga is discussed

seudah - meal

sofer- scribe

selichos - penitence service ten days before *Rosh Hashanah*

Shabbos - *Sabbath* (pl: *Shabbosim*), Saturday

shalom - peace, also a word of greeting and farewell

shalom bayis - peace in the home; domestic harmony

shanda - shame

Shavuos - the holiday that commemorates receiving the *Torah* on Mt. Sinai

sheitel - wig

sheva brochos - the seven blessings said under the *chuppah* and after the completion of the wedding meal; also parties held for the bride and groom for seven nights after the wedding

shidduch- the introduction of a boy and girl to each other for the purpose of matrimony

shiva - the week of mourning after a death

shlosh seudos - third meal on the Sabbath day

shmatte - derogatory term for a dress, literally a "rag"

shul - synagogue

shulchon aruch - code of law

simcha - a joyful event, a wedding, a *bris*, etc.

Simchas Torah - festive, happy holiday when Jews finish reading the last book of the Five Books of Moses (Deuteronomy), and then immediately start reading *Genesis* again

succah - a booth or hut used during the holiday of *Succos*

Succos- holiday that commemorates the journey through the desert when the Jews lived in booths

talmid chochom - a knowledgeable and wise student of *Torah*

talmid teepash - a fool

taharat hamishpacha - laws of family purity

tashlich - the symbolic casting away of sins near a body of water during the New Year (Rosh Hashanah)

tenayim - engagement contract

Tisha B'av- a sad day when our two temples were destroyed (a fast day)

Torah- the Five Books of Moses

tzedakah- charity

yasher koach- may you go from strength to strength

yenta - busybody

yerusha - inheritance

yeshiva - school for Orthodox children where the curriculum includes English and Judaic studies.

yichud room - set aside for the bride and groom to have a few minutes of privacy and a bite to eat after the wedding ceremony

yom tov - Jewish holiday, literally "good day" (pl: *yomim tovim*)

yontif - Yiddish for Jewish holiday

zadekes - a wise, charitable, righteous woman

zivug - pre-destined mate

zocheh - merit